ALAN BROWNJOHN is well known
he received a Lifetime Achievemer
Guild of Great Britain in 2007. Born in 1931, he was educated at
Merton College, Oxford and worked as a teacher and lecturer
for twenty-five years. He has been a freelance writer and
broadcaster since 1978, publishing four novels (including the
prizewinning *The Way You Tell Them* in 1990, and *Windows on the
Moon* in 2009), and has reviewed poetry for the *New Statesman,
Encounter* and *The Sunday Times*. Eleven individual volumes of
verse were represented in his *Collected Poems* (Enitharmon Press,
2006), and a twelfth, *Ludbrooke and Others*, followed in 2010.
The Saner Places contains his personal choice of poems from all
of these books.

Alan Brownjohn

THE SANER PLACES
SELECTED POEMS

ENITHARMON PRESS

First published in 2011
by Enitharmon Press
26B Caversham Road
London NW5 2DU

www.enitharmon.co.uk

Distributed in the UK by
Central Books
99 Wallis Road
London E9 5LN

Distributed in the USA and Canada
by Dufour Editions Inc.
PO Box 7, Chester Springs
PA 19425, USA

ISBN: 978-1-907587-07-8

Enitharmon Press gratefully acknowledges the
financial support of Arts Council England.

British Library Cataloguing-in-Publication Data.
A catalogue record for this book is available
from the British Library.

Designed in Albertina by Libanus Press
and printed in England by
Antony Rowe Ltd

for Kate and Steve

ACKNOWLEDGEMENTS

In my three editions of *Collected Poems* (1983, 1988 and 2006) the poems were allocated to the decades in which they were written (1950s, 1960s, etc.) and not listed under the titles of the individual volumes in which they were originally published. I have dropped the custom for this first *Selected Poems*, and named all of those books from *The Railings* (1961) onwards.

It has thus seemed an appropriate point at which to thank by name the editors who made them possible, and for whose encouragement and care I am deeply grateful: Peter Digby Smith, Kevin Crossley-Holland, Anthony Thwaite, Anthony Whittome, Christopher Sinclair-Stevenson, and Stephen Stuart-Smith at Enitharmon Press who has now enabled me to bring back into circulation with this *Selected* poems from several out-of-print volumes.

A small number of slightly longer poems (for example, 'A Night in the Gazebo' in the book given that title, and 'The Seventh Knight and the Green Cat' from the same volume) were difficult to excerpt, and so are not represented. Three much longer sequences are represented by a small selection from each; they are 'A Song of Good Life', 'Sea Pictures' and 'The Automatic Days'. All of these five may be found in my 2006 *Collected Poems*.

A.B.

CONTENTS

From THE MEN AROUND HER BED (2004)

From COLLECTED POEMS (2006)

From LUDBROOKE AND OTHERS (2010)

Ludbrooke

And Others

FROM
THE RAILINGS
(1961)

Two Poems from Prévert

'IN THIS CITY . . .'

In this city, perhaps a street.
In this street, perhaps a house.
In this house, perhaps a room
And in this room a woman sitting,
Sitting in the darkness, sitting and crying
For someone who has just gone through the door
And who has just switched off the light
Forgetting she was there.

'WE ARE GOING TO SEE THE RABBIT . . .'

We are going to see the rabbit,
We are going to see the rabbit.
Which rabbit, people say?
Which rabbit, ask the children?
Which rabbit?
The only rabbit,
The only rabbit in England,
Sitting behind a barbed-wire fence
Under the floodlights, neon lights,
Sodium lights,
Nibbling grass
On the only patch of grass
In England, in England
(Except the grass by the hoardings
Which doesn't count.)
We are going to see the rabbit
And we must be there on time.

First we shall go by escalator,
Then we shall go by underground,
And then we shall go by motorway
And then by helicopterway,
And the last ten yards we shall have to go
On foot.

And now we are going
All the way to see the rabbit,
We are nearly there,
We are longing to see it,
And so is the crowd
Which is here in thousands
With mounted policemen
And big loudspeakers
And bands and banners,
And everyone has come a long way.

But soon we shall see it
Sitting and nibbling
The blades of grass
On the only patch of grass
In – but something has gone wrong!
Why is everyone so angry,
Why is everyone jostling
And slanging and complaining?

The rabbit has gone,
Yes, the rabbit has gone.
He has actually burrowed down into the earth
And made himself a warren, under the earth,
Despite all these people.
And what shall we do?
What *can* we do?

It is all a pity, you must be disappointed,
Go home and do something else for today,
Go home again, go home for today.
For you cannot hear the rabbit, under the earth,
Remarking rather sadly to himself, by himself,
As he rests in his warren, under the earth:
'It won't be long, they are bound to come,
They are bound to come and find me, even here.'

WILLIAM EMPSON AT ALDERMASTON

This is our dead sea, once a guidebook heath.
Left and right hands worked busily together
A parliament or two,
And there she stands:

Twelve miles of cooling pipes; concrete and secret
Warrens underground; clean little towers
Clamped with strong ladders; red, brisk vans
Which hurry round

The wide, kerbed avenues with pulsing lights
To signify danger; and all this
Extending still its miles, as seas possessed
Of power or anger

Will – except that here
The tide decrees, with threats in yellow paint,
Its own unquestioned bounds, keeps dogs to catch
Someone who gets

Beyond the fence: it seems that otherwise
We shiver from an unclean nakedness,
And need to clothe our hot emotions cold
With wire, and curs.

But let there be some praise, where that is due:
For paint, of enlivening colours, spent
On all these deathly offices.Where typists sit,
Who do not make the thing,

Or scientists, who do not fire the thing,
Or workers, who obey the scientists,
The rooms are beautiful. And anyone
Who passed by car one day

Not knowing what it was would never guess.
(Perhaps some urgent public undertaking
Set up for health, or water? Or a camp
Where other people went

On holidays?) Such airs of carnival,
With death designed as smiling, to conceal
His proper features – these things justified
Replies in kind:

An absurd fête of life, in one Friday field
For which no pass was needed. The effect:
Two sorts of carnival clashing: on this side
The mud, or grass,

The boots and stoves and caravans; that side,
The trim, discreet pavilions of the State.
And one more contrast marked these gaieties:
This side there seemed

Some thousands, while of death's there wasn't one.
Just the white-braided police returned the stare
Of the boys with haversacks, or the fierce
Empirical gaze

Of the man with the Chinese beard, or the pondering glance
Of the woman with the basket on wheels.
And some thought death's precise executives
Had told or asked

The servants of his will to stay away,
Hinting of jobs they might not like to lose,
And they had houses . . . from whose windows, next,
Many faces looked the way

Of the procession; speaking not a word,
But merely watching. How else, then, explain
If this was not the reason, why their children,
Through all the bands and singing,

All the beards and the guitars, did not come out;
But stood behind held curtains, listlessly,
With tight and puzzled faces, or peered through
Some furtive upstairs sunblind

While it passed? No coloured hat, not one
In all the range of shirts and slogans worn,
Seemed odder than these faces. That deep blankness
Was the real thing strange.

THE RAILINGS

Once there would have been the woman standing
Between the trees behind the dancing railings as he walked,
But that is not now so.

And once there would have been
A hope of the woman, a figment of the branches
As they shifted with the light –
That might have been, that might have been,
But neither is this any longer true.

Not even now is the hope what it was,
And will not regain the face:
Two years, three years, the walk could go
While only the principle of the woman

Faintly remained. And that would scarcely be enough.
The principle will drain from out a place.
The hope will have to go to other things.

A GARDEN IN SUMMER

August is skilful in erasing fear,
And out of the full greenhouse into sunlight
I have now followed mine down the terraces
To find nothing where shore and garden meet.

On a clear sea's day it has no place,
Vanished, or simplified in the slanting light
Or under the mild oaks' shadows that turn
From shade to dusk. No place, that is, until

The absence of dread, pure sense of bondage broken, is itself
The burden feared, the freedom threatened suddenly.
And in a consciousness of joy the fear returns,
Fear that its wholeness must be too complete, its passing

Begin where even now the trees are still,
The air grows cold, a summer's tide drains out,
Horizons approach with the closeness of cloud,
And the slow warm wind through the garden falters, dies.

FOR A JOURNEY

House Field, Top Field, Oak Field, Third Field:
Though maps conclude their duties, the names trek on
Unseen across every county. Farmers call hillocks
And ponds and streams and lanes and rocks
By the first words to hand; a heavy, whittled-down
Simplicity meets the need, enough to help say
Where has yielded best, or the way they walked from home.

You can travel safely over land so named –
Where there is nowhere that could not somewhere
Be found in a memory which knows, and loves.
So watch then, all the more carefully, for
The point where the pattern ends: where mountains, even,
And swamps and forests and gaping bays acquire
The air of not needing ever to be spoken of.

Who knows what could become of you where
No one has understood the place with names?

THE LIONS' MOUTHS
(1967)

ODE TO FELIX

At that tired eye-level point where
Impulse buying starts, he
Was there in flush, banked rows in
The supermarket: Felix the Cat.

Two dozen cat-food packets, patterned
For sales appeal, repeated two
Dozen static gestures of his face who
Almost first made cartoons animate.

I remembered that black-and-white
Stroll, brought back on the t.v. screen
About twenty years after: undoubtedly
Smart for its time, the commentator said.

Yes, he had all the possibilities
Already, little early Felix. His
Famous walk was even then the quaint, quick
Cartoon swagger, his features were

The easy prototype of all
Those smirking descendants, capering
In slick, flourished lines, richer
For the primary colours, and running on

Down and down a million celluloid frames
Hand-painted in endless studio rows by
Patient, paid artists reducing everything to
That clear-cut, lucid world, while

Elsewhere other grown men sound-tracked
The basic squawk. – This way was
The world infested by your
Charming animal kingdom, Felix, having

Driven out real beasts. Numberless
American children responded to
The uncle-funny voices, actually came
To look like Mickey Mouse. In the

Demure eyes of innumerable
Homely girls and wives lived
Bambi's primal innocence. Felix,
You were first of all those lovably

Blundering and resourceless dogs and
Elephants who helped to make our
Gross and failing natures bearable.
You set off Li'l Abner, firm and strait,

Shouldering over fields with no effort, as in
Our own fulfilment dreams, you
Tamed with Snow White all our dwarfs
And witches, you helped to paint

Donald Duck on the fuselage of
The bomber for Hiroshima. If today
A man in the *Sunday Times* Colour
Supplement makes t.v. commercials

To pay to make his very own cartoon
Satirizing agencies, the credit's
Partly yours, and you can be proud to think your
Walt Disney voted for Goldwater . . .

I would not buy your food, I have no cat.
I can pass on down the stacked and shining
Aisles to other violences (the frozen red
Chops glossed in cellophane on puce, plastic trays)

But I'm not to pass without that sense, again,
Of one of my more elementary sorts of
Going mad: Your thousands of representatives,
Felix, walking into my world, writing my

Morning letters, modulating from the shapes
Of strangers outside the house, answering
My alarm calls for Fire, Police, *Ambulance*. In
That last nightmare trap and maze, they

Strut and chirp their obscene, unstoppable
Platitudes, Felix, while I run round and
Round and round to destroy their pert, joking smiles
And scream my own voice hoarse into their cute squeak.

1939

Where the ball ran into the bushes,
And I was sent to find it, being
Useful for that more than to play their game,
I saw instead
This badge, from someone's brother, in
Some regiment of that war: a trophy
Begged for and polished, coveted certainly,
But lost now, slightly touched with dust already,
Yet shining still, under smooth leaves drab with dust.
I knew that people prized such trophies then,
It was the way of all of us. I might,
For no one looked, have taken it
For mine. I valued it. It shone
For me as much as anyone.
And yet some fear or honesty, some sense
It wasn't to be mine – it wasn't more –

Said No to all of this. Besides,
They shouted in the distance for their ball.
For once quite quickly, I
Made up my mind
And left the thing behind.

CLASS INCIDENT FROM GRAVES

Wednesdays were guest night in the mess, when the colonel
expected the married officers, who usually dined at home, to attend.
The band played Gilbert and Sullivan music behind a curtain. . . .
Afterwards the bandmaster was invited to the senior officers' table
for his complimentary glass of Light or Vintage.

(Good-bye to All That)

At the officers' table, for half an hour afterwards, port,
The bandmaster. He accepts, one drink long,
All the courtesy of the gentlemen. They are suave, and equal.
'I expect with your job . . . Do you find . . . Oh well . . .'
The bandmaster edges the shining inch of port along the grain
 of the table,
Precisely covering one knot with the transparent
Base of the glass. He crouches forward over the polished wood
Towards the officers, not comfortably convivial,
Eyes always going to the face speaking next,
Deferential, very pleased.
The band put away their instruments out at the back, having
Drunk their beers, standing.
The detachable pieces of brass lie down
In the felt grooves of the cases, just as they should.
Nine-thirty strikes.
There is laughter of men together, coming from inside.
'Mitchell's still in there, hob-nobbing with the officers.'

OFFICE PARTY

We were throwing out small-talk
On the smoke-weary air,
When the girl with the squeaker
Came passing each chair.

She was wearing a white dress,
Her paper-hat was a blue
Crown with a red tassel,
And to every man who

Glanced up at her, she leant over
And blew down the hole,
So the squeaker inflated
And began to unroll.

She stopped them all talking
With this trickery,
And she didn't leave out anyone
Until she came to me.

I looked up and she met me
With a half-teasing eye
And she took a mild breath and
Went carefully by,

And with cold concentration
To the next man she went,
And squawked out the instrument
To its fullest extent.

And whether she passed me
Thinking that it would show
Too much favour to mock me
I never did know –

Or whether her withholding
Was her cruelty,
And it was that she despised me,
I couldn't quite see –

So it could have been discretion,
And it could have been disgust,
But it was quite unequivocal,
And suffer it I must:

All I know was: she passed me,
Which I did not expect
– And I'd never so craved for
Some crude disrespect.

FARMER'S POINT OF VIEW

I own certain acre-scraps of woodland, scattered
On undulating ground; enough to lie hidden in. So,

About three times a year, and usually August,
Pairs of people come to one or another patch. They stray

Around the edges first, plainly wanting some excuse
To go on in; then talking, as if not concerned,

And always of something else, not what they intend,
They find their way, by one or another approach,

To conducting sexual liaisons – on *my* land.
I've tried to be careful. I haven't mentioned 'love'

Or any idea of passion or consummation;
And I won't call them 'lovers' because I can't say

If they come from affection, or lust, or blackmail,
Or if what they do has any particular point

For either or both (and who can say what 'love' means?)
So what am I saying? I'd like to see people pondering

What unalterable acts they might be committing
When they step down, full of plans, from their trains or cars.

I am not just recording their tragic, or comic, emotions,
Or even the subtler hazards of owning land –

I am honestly concerned. I want to say, politely,
That I worry when I think what they're about:

I want them to explain themselves before they use my woods.

THE SPACE

Then why see it? This 'flat and ample
Space over which you walk at no one angle,
Led as by something very like your will?'

*You could go on with proper concerns. You
Are boiling tea, typing some letter, listening
To politics when it comes. Why let it, why let*

It come? – That pale, clean stretch
Stays small, and won't usurp the whole. So
I let it come. There is no harmful freedom.

But where do you go across that space? Do you
See things, see anyone? I don't go anywhere
But across it; taut and clear, though the wind leans at me.

Further, it might be a world, and not safe:
It might be stayed in. I keep it unfulfilled.
Its colour? Certain shadows, shades of green.

– And whoever she who walks there, and stands,
She won't tremble into definition, isn't
Like Fournier's girl, say, on the steps and real.

Then why let it come at all? Only, that to this
All common facts yearn to approximate,
While time strains to reach it. And it

Won't be otherwise, it refuses, and must
Return as plainly as before; nothing but
A kind of sober walking-space. – I see

You are not answered why, nor sense why I let it come.

FROM

SANDGRAINS ON A TRAY
(1969)

HEDONIST

It was not the religious pleasure-principle,
The supposed, long quest of the libertine; nor
Was it any kind of arrant desire for
Immolation in some seizing mode of brief
Forgetfulness. It was no sort of strained belief,
Or meditated act; but much more simple:

It was the sense of the sufficient good-ness
Of the next thing beyond the present thing:
The food after a day not eating,
The landing after the stairs, the prospect of some
Prospect filling the ten next minutes, should they come.
It was sleep, sometimes. But simpler even than these,

It could be just the sunlight, as an amiable event
To walk out into after the thick
Complexities of his room, leaving cigarettes, stick
And tablets and trusting, for once,
To his own feet and the friendliness of distance,
And to mere walking alone on the bright pavement.

BALLS OF SWEETNESS

Before James Carra knew Anne Furlington
She made love, often, the first in both their lives,
Under a slipping mauve quilt in a seaport,
With nightlong traffic noise disturbing;
There being wallpaper the same as in her
College room; and it was Peter Daines.
It was the world. No one seemed later hurt, or
Finally betrayed.
                    It was not of consequence.

When Hester Lang told Cavan Benther that
Hidden in some long spell away from him was
A week when Philip Quernier was prepared
And it happened three times (but each time one of them
Pretended) an hour was enough for Cavan's
Fury. Nor were these people heartless. It was
Not of consequence. Such oddness at such distance
Could be healed.
                    It was the world.

Elizabeth Pender felt that past could be
Contentedly left as past concerning
William Stennett's beds where Margaret Bourn
Fought conscience and hindering fear. She
Only nodded; and thought. Such guileless frankness
Gave a lot of help. This would leave
No injury-traces . . . It was the world. In minutes
Their hands came coolly together.
                                    It was not of consequence.

A 202

    This coarse road, my road, struggles out
    South-east across London, an exhausted
    Grey zigzag of stubborn, unassimilable
        Macadam, passing hoardings pasted

    With blow-ups of cricket journalists, blackened
    And not-quite-Georgian terraces,
    Shagged-out Greens of geraniums and
        Floral coats-of-arms, lost pieces

Of genteel façade behind and above
Lyons' shopfronts and 'Pullum Promotions',
– Journeying between wired-off bombed lots glossy
    With parked Consuls, making diversions

Round bus depots and draggled estates
In circumlocutory One-Ways,
Netting aquaria in crammed pet store windows,
    Skirting multi-racial bingo queues,

And acquiring, for its self-hating hoard, old black-railed
Underground bogs advising the Seamen's Hospital,
'Do-it-yourself' shops, 'Funerals and Monuments', and
    Victorian Charrington pubs. All

Along its length it despoils, in turn, a sequence
Of echoless names: Camberwell, Peckham,
New Cross Gate; places having no recorded past
    Except in histories of the tram.

It takes out, in cars, arterial affluence
At week-ends, returning it as bad blood
To Monday mornings in town. It is altogether
    Like a vein travelled by hardy diseases, an aged

Canal dredgeable for bodies left behind
On its soulless travels: Sixty-Nine,
Thirty-Six, One-Eight-Five. It takes no clear
    Attitude anyone could easily define

So as to resist or admire it. It seems to hate you
Possessively, want to envelop you in nothing
Distinguishable or distinguished, like its own
    Smothered slopes and rotting

Valleys. This road, generally, is one for
The long-defeated; and turns any ironic
Observer's tracer-isotope of ecology,
    Sociology, or hopeful manic

Verse into a kind of mere
Nosing virus itself. It leaves its despondent, foul
And intractable deposit on its own
    Banks all the way like virtually all

Large rivers, particularly the holy ones, which it
Is not. It sees little that deserves to be undespised.
It only means well in the worst of ways.
    How much of love is much less compromised?

THE CLOUDS

The craftsmen in my line bred out.
I drive, but could I mend a fuse.
My fathers handled founts of words
My brain would catch and fingers lose.

I find a fair excuse, to serve:
There has, in our society,
Been 'social change', which makes these skills
Much less of a necessity.

Beyond your shoulder I can see
A saucer – stamped out by machine –
On the formica shelf near where
We lie on quilts of terylene.

No sort of ancient expertise
Goes to create these modern things:
To them, no craftsman's hand its pride
Or love for their completeness brings.

Their very make and feel rejects
Any thought that such loving powers
Nurtured their shapes to what they are
Through someone's calm and patient hours.

That care seems obsolete. – Yes, I know
You were your parents' artefact,
Your perfect head, shoulders and back
Made in a sort-of skilful act,

But when I move a care-ful hand
(No craftsman's art its legacy)
And dot a pattering line to count
Your poised and tensing vertebrae,

It's not *great* numeracy I want,
Or flair for cold technologies
– Such details are not wanted in
All kinds of loving enterprise.

Nor do we need such skills to lose
All sense of this room, house and street . . .
And don't doubt, though we use no craft,
That love it is makes this complete.

– And, well, on looking up I see,
As a sweet end to summer's drought,
Some wholly unskilled clouds which pour
Blessings of rain on Baron's Court.

SOMEHOW

The North Lancashire Ballet Group is coming
Next month, and Miriam Granger-White is giving
A Francis Thompson reading in the Public
Library. So we are all well catered for, culture-wise,
And don't really miss London. It's interesting
How many talented people do in fact
Choose the provinces: you seem to get
Room to breathe here somehow, and so many

Advantages (for instance, the post for London
Goes as late as *eleven* on weekdays!).We have these
Musician friends – the husband's often having things
Done by the choir of Radio Chesterfield, the wife
Lectures in a College of Education – they're like us,
They gave up London because it just didn't seem
To offer the scope somehow. Robert's work is
Going awfully well; as I think I told you, it's

An open-minded, progressive sort of firm, and he has
The chance to do a small, quite modern, country
Cottage for a retired solicitor. He's pretty sure
The standard is as high as a lot of firms
In London. I do several hours each week
Helping at the Family Planning Clinic, there's plenty
To occupy us. Yes, we keep in touch, we can
Get most of our old friends on S.T.D.,

And people really do exaggerate about the northern
Weather. I wouldn't at all like to have
To drive the Anglia in London traffic. I don't think
I could. There's a design shop in the Market Square
Where you can get almost anything, a delicatessen

With every kind of bread we like, and
A fabric shop as good as Oxford Street. Robert
Is on the Third Programme Listeners' Panel.

We are growing lobelias for the local Help the Depressives
Flower Show, which keeps us busy. It's
A good life.Would you like to come down?
We have an enormous spare room and it would
Be lovely to see you. You could stay as long as
You like – we wouldn't bother you. It's
Quite possible, don't you think, to be 'provincial'
While actually living in the metropolis? Anyway,

Write soon, tell us your news, love to Amanda.

COMMON SENSE

An agricultural labourer, who has
A wife and four children, receives 20s a week.
3/4 buys food, and the members of the family
Have three meals a day.
How much is that per person per meal?
   – *From Pitman's Common Sense Arithmetic, 1917*

A gardener, paid 24s a week, is
Fined 1/3 if he comes to work late.
At the end of 26 weeks, he receives
£30.5.3. How
Often was he late?
   – *From Pitman's Common Sense Arithmetic, 1917*

A milk dealer buys milk at 3*d* a quart. He
Dilutes it with 3% water and sells
124 gallons of the mixture at
4*d* per quart. How much of his profit is made by
Adulterating the milk?

 — From Pitman's Common Sense Arithmetic, 1917

The table printed below gives the number
Of paupers in the United Kingdom, and
The total cost of poor relief.
Find the average number
Of paupers per ten thousand people.

 — From Pitman's Common Sense Arithmetic, 1917

An army had to march to the relief of
A besieged town, 500 miles away, which
Had telegraphed that it could hold out for 18 days.
The army made forced marches at the rate of 18
Miles a day. Would it be there in time?

 — From Pitman's Common Sense Arithmetic, 1917

Out of an army of 28,000 men,
15% were
Killed, 25% were
Wounded. Calculate
How many men there were left to fight.

 — From Pitman's Common Sense Arithmetic, 1917

These sums are offered to
That host of young people in our Elementary Schools, who
Are so ardently desirous of setting
Foot upon the first rung of the
Educational ladder . . .

 — From Pitman's Common Sense Arithmetic, 1917

Oliver Cromwell and Beethoven both
Died in the middle of thunderstorms. Ruth
Didn't know this, but knew Kierkegaard's Dad
Cursed God from a hilltop, or so it was said.
Yet none of these things was at all familiar
To Mary, or Nora, or Helen, or Pamela.

But Pamela knew of some laws of Justinian's,
Helen listened to Schutz and had read *The Virginians*,
And Nora and Mary liked Wallace Stevens,
So in general terms it worked out evens
– Except that none of them, only Amanda,
Knew that Oliver Cromwell had died during thunder.

Still, here were these women with items of knowledge
Picked up in one and another college
– And here am I with not quite all their gaps
In my knowledge of all these high-powered chaps,
Doing well with the female population
And their limited but charming conversation.

WARRIOR'S CAREER

(1972)

ODE TO MELANCHOLY
(*for Martin Bell*)

I have made England
almost
unusable with associations. Every

beach, square, terrace or
shattered chancel has its
touchy girl, saying

'Don't go back *there*.'
                              So
on Bank Holiday I walk
home, home in the sun. Little

cats jump their heads into
my hand, but I can't talk
to *people*. Closing

my door, it's eight hours
playing and refining the
games of melancholia:

cushions, records,
crumbling sugar-heaps,
self-love. O gentle, helpful

melancholy, give me
one good doodle on a
white page for

all my afternoon's journey;
rescind time's
importance for me so I don't

care how the days of the week are
seven, the days of the month are
seven plus twenty-one; and

feed me black coffee, black
cigarettes, black socks
(toujours

la délicatesse!) – that I can
wait so happily for
darkness to require

all those curtains to be pulled.

THE PACKET

In the room,
In the woman's hand as she turns
Is the packet of salt.

On the packet is a picture of a
Woman turning,
With a packet in her hand.

When the woman in the room com-
Pletes her turning, she
Puts the packet down and leaves.

On the packet in the picture
Is: a picture of a woman
Turning, with a packet in her hand.

On this packet is a picture: of a woman,
Turning, with a packet in her hand.
On this packet is no picture

– It is a tiny blank.
                    And now the man waits,
And waits: two-thirty, seven-thirty,
Twelve.

At twelve he lays the packet on its side
And draws, in the last packet in the last
Picture, a tiny woman turning.

And then he locks the door,
And switches off the bedside lamp,
And among the grains of salt he goes to sleep.

CONNECTION

The first take was an offer in eagerness,
With every white finger so quickly threading,
Those hands went on as if they didn't think.

But they thought for the second take; which was
A slow agreed advancing, and a
Watching with eyes to see what eyes would tell.

The third take was from longer forethought, becoming
A turmoil and grating of little, decorated
Bones; neither hand wanted it.
                              In fact,

The fourth take might never have been at all,
Except. . . . some kind of separateness travelled
The arm to the shoulder, the shoulder to the brain

And there it spoke: to separate, such hands
Needed to have been joined
                              and been confused
– Once more those fingers did as they were used.

BALLAD OF SCARLET AND BLACK

Waking at her lover's knocking, or
So she thought, she crossed, running,
A carpet twenty yards wide
To the curtains at the window, scarlet-
And-black,
And drew them.

Or so she thought.
                        Because
Behind the first curtains were
More curtains, and behind
The second were third,
And behind the third were fourth, none
Of them opening into daylight and onto
Her lover's face waiting at her door,
But onto only
Scarlet-and-black and then
Scarlet-and-black and then
Scarlet-and-black.
But several seconds later truly waking,
She drew

The curtains which were not in her dream,
And were one foot from her bed,
And were scarlet-and-black
And let straight daylight immediately in.

So now she combed, at her mirror, with
Fingers over open eyes, a parting in her hair, counting
Which day of daylight this was, and counting
The years of her life again.

And when her lover called, she
Went across town with him talking of her dream
      and what it meant,
Talking of their parting, and joining, and their
      endless counting of time,
And she was trying, trying to uncover
His daylight face.

Up the stairs to his room,
Their blood was the blood of veins returning to the heart,
Returning as if with ritual nostalgia to the heart,
Between scarlet and black.
There, pulling the black,

Lying under the scarlet, curtains, unhooked from the wall,
They made again the love of years,
With his face in darkness;
And then, with fingers across closed eyes
She sorted apart her hair
And slept until the next daylight arrived to be counted.

PASTORAL

Some pining cows – with unenchanted sniffing –
Browsed the wan grass. Straggles of green wheat lay
Thrown down by ill-conditioned winds near where
A river dragged past, in a surly way.

Between two stony, grubby settlements,
There was a bend in a connecting lane
Providing, helpfully, some pallid verges,
And here the foxhunt met, in spraying rain.

Sound flesh and arteries swelled boldly outwards
Over the confident bones; the usual
Red coats and leather trouserings were sported;
Their little caps were the identical

Hunt gear for anywhere; and each man had
A placid piebald which, as he proudly sat,
Fumed feathery steam from nostrils set in faces
Looking well-pleased to do what they were at.

An indoor lighting, very blue and feeble
– A sort-of paintwork of the high sky-shell –
Fell on the hounds, brought up in snarling batches
And loving it, so far as one could tell.

Then, at a billowing horn-call from the master,
Each creature fled off, with a huge sultry bound
After a prey let fly for their pursuing
And chased across a grey and powdery ground.

In all these men and women pride was burning
To have this ceremony in such a place:
The air-locked air smelt grand, the beasts were sprightly,
The clothes were filled with arrogance and grace.

The faces, just as furious and paltry
As were their ancestors' before their births,
Joyed at the springy touch of lunar pastures
As had those solid forebears' on the earth's.

If some forebears had dared to be the first ones,
And radioed back, and from a special bag
Took cameras to photograph each other
And set them up a little national flag,

And gave rehearsed extempore impressions
Of how it felt on their historic day,
And walked around collecting bits and pieces
On screens two hundred thousand miles away,

All this was so that natural human measures
Could dance themselves wherever men might be,
With nothing fine or beautiful neglected,
And nowhere closed to oafish liberty.

PROJECTION

And that midnight raced across
Down the sand, James Carra first. And
Though the air drenched his eyes,
Suddenly he saw the thing, the figure, his
Own shadow running terribly forwards onto

Him, out of the water; because all these four
People were running straight down the
Headlight path in the dark to the shallow
Sea, and had met their ghosts rearing
Up from the tide-edge. Where

The water stood them, the four stood
In quiet and disquiet, trying to trace
The invisible lip of the retrenching
Tide. The sea was unseizably dark.
This distance, the car lights couldn't

Choose out one wave-crest; but then the water
Was blankly calm where the four
Stopped, and couldn't speak, before
Their huge grey shapes hovering
And diffusing upon the Atlantic. Such

Ghosts they were content to own,
Knowing their nature, the un-
Measurable powerlessness of shadows. And when
They turned back up their glaring track
Those vast greynesses comfortingly

Dwindled again (slowly, because they walked)
Dwindled into the sea again, that did
Nothing. Only James Carra, walking,
Thought more than this, as he measured out the
Dark sand and caught at his disrupted breath

— As he knew she would catch, who
Lay across the water in the
Drowning sheets, checking her
Breath for a lover on whom no
Writs or shadows he could cast could run.

FROM
A SONG OF GOOD LIFE
(1975)

INTERVIEW WITH A CREATOR

No, not the idea of slamming at people with the stone
From the start.

We begin with the product itself,
And make it into something which people can be persuaded
To want of their own free will.
What we do is, we adapt
The image of the stone.

Take this picture of the stone in the Supplement,
The grain of its firm arm around the brunette
On the undulating fields of County Down.

– Or, if you like,
We soften the stone.

Between the News and the Quiz the
Giggling little rubber stone frisks
And carols around the screen
With a backing of sweet music from a combo
Of pliant pebbles.
A voice confesses:
I never bought any other stone since I first tried this.

Walking the outspread supermarket glades, Mrs Bourn
Sees the price reduced on the turquoise packaging
Round the offer of succulent stones. And some stones
Nestle in her tray at the check-out instead of bread.

Two minutes only in lightly-salted water,
And they slip down the smiling throats at the table
With no trouble at all.

Mrs Bourn's young family of seven can't wait
For their dainty stones.

ARRANGED BLOSSOMS

Peeling itself away like a morsel of skin,
There's another petal to be seen to,
Deranging the antique order of the room.

She must get Mr Fernlock to cast her again.
Knowing the right things to do, the investments,
The Settlement, the family, is so hard.

Angela can be so very hard.
One can't give straight advice as one can face-to-face
When the two of them are in Johannesburg.

Well, I can't stand the weather here either.
But this is my home; and Angela,
You might try writing more often than you do.

Dust the Wedgwood now, not later, it's waited two days.
She must get herself cast again, horoscopes
Can alter for the better, she has heard this.

Tuesday already, and so much to do before Friday.
Friday is the car to Mr Goodman's
To get the codicil witnessed.

And things going wrong she can't manage herself,
Yes, that tap thumping ever since last Thursday week.
A dirty man, who smoked, and it still won't stop.

VITAL

I think my work is important, I am a link
In a long chain.
I had to have the training for it,
And I had to dirty my hands.
They ask my advice when they want to know what would be
best.

I might move up even higher, in time.

One Sunday I woke up shouting. She said,
What on earth's the matter, we're supposed to be
Going out to dinner later; or rather lunch.
I dressed, and played with Lynda, and
Felt a bit better.

I was called into the office from the shop
Floor. 'Mr Fletton, up from London, wants to see you.'
But I was hearing the mutter-mutter,
The kind-of giggling noises inside the machines
Through four thick concrete walls.
I could not read the words in front of my eyes.

She said last Thursday, you haven't said a thing
The whole evening.
I said no, I've been watching.
. . . I couldn't name a thing I'd seen on the screen.

Today is vital, people are relying on me
To get ten thousand packages out on time.
I am part of a chain, a link, they ask my advice.
I open the front door. After the wind,
It's a lovely cool morning, and sun;
Very bright.

The keys of the Toledo are clenched wet
In my right hand. And I don't move.
I am standing shaking. I am standing, shaking.

THE SHIP OF DEATH

First, prolonged and weird estuarial waters,
　　And so wide before you realise: full of rusted,
Sunken, purposeless objects; or creaking guide-lights
　　Offering unclear channels, curving paths
Of a grey water greyer than the rest. And now the eager
　　Sea-birds that followed have dropped back for the shore.
The strip-lighting blinks on in the Dining Room, the cutlery
　　Scintillates. But you don't enjoy their small-talk at the table, as
The white-coated band on the platform lilts into selections,
　　Selections: it's a musical about your life they
Are playing them from, and it could not have run long in town.
　　Now the ship tilts, and the crockery slides downhill; and
There is a tannoy announcement from the captain:
　　Welcoming you to the ship, hoping you will be
Comfortable, and reminding you there is no destination.
　　You leave the table for the bar. Already it's dark, which
Might be more interesting; though you expected, looking out,
　　That a scattering of stars might show; and the sky's dull.
Far off, is it west, you can pick out an esplanade
　　With lights like a frippery of beads; you
Never attained that one, wherever. Your drink hasn't lasted,
　　The print in your newspaper blurs and you can't see faces
Very clearly. The map, of the route of the ship in
　　The frame on the wall, is practically blank. Is there a rest
　　　　　　　　　　　　　　　　　　　　　　　　　　　room?

The stewards don't attend to you, they are attending
    To the bed-makers in the cabins. The duty-free shop
Is a shut grille. The handrail in the corridor misses
    Your hand, upstairs both sides of the deck cant you into
The bullets of the spray. The wake is dark, the prow is
                                                chained off.
    You go to the Engine Room for the monotone of the
                                                drone,
But that is no anaesthetic. There should be
    Amusements aboard, surely? What about the staterooms
Looking so sumptuous in the brochures? And the gilt lounges?
    Something worth having this ticket for? God, this ship feels
No different from being alive; because
    Your seaboard walk shakes like your walk on land, and
All your thinking ends at the same advice: it's time, no
    Other choice, to go down the metal steps to
Where it says Men, and lock the door; be alone, alone,
    You may find, there, what's wrong that you couldn't
Name, that nobody found out.
                                – So this you do, except
    That when you have closed the door, the door locks
On you. Rust runs in lifelong trickles from the welded
    Bolts of this cubicle; everything shudders, even more,
In you and the whole ship. No hammering for help,
    Or calling, it's H.M.S. Death, death: the eternal
Accumulated store of everything life became: just
    Yourself, as you are, and your face in that bowl. Smile,
                                                you're free
To vomit your self-regard for the rest of the voyage.

APRIL FOOL'S CAROL

Celebrate today belladonna and shot silk.
Women will do what they are for.

Belladonna: poisons in
Certain quantities are a cure.
Women will do what they are for.

Shot silk: it changes at a look, you move
It varies, contrary; but
Is completely one, its feel
Will rub the best and nothing, ever, more.
Women will do what they are for.

The Marys are at every birth, and grave
Delivery, at every marriage too they wear
Their ancient finery: *Women*
('Sing all a green . . .')
                    Will do what they are for.

OF DANCING

My dancing is, in my opinion, good,
In the right, cramped circumstances, and provided
Other people are too preoccupied with
Their own to notice mine. I am happy
To have lived into an informal age when
Standing and shaking in approximate rhythm, not
Bowing and guiding, is the idea. Because to
Have to know regulated steps and be skilful was what
I could never manage at all when it was the thing.

So I do dance. But I'm never entirely sure.
It's a kind of movement you would never make
In the normal course, and how much it always seems
To obtrude on the natural in an embarrassing
Way wherever people get it started!
Set it apart, on a stage, with a large
Orchestra, it's all right, it's undoubtedly clever,
And the costumes are glorious to gawp at, but
It still looks a little bit foolish, moving like *that?*

To speak of how all its origins are so
Utterly primal - the planets, the seasons,
The rhythms of mating, and so on, and so on,
Is to list a lot of fundamental things,
Explain them, and exorcise dancing:
Because simply why dance if you've come to understand
What dancing mimes so roughly, or makes such
A repetitive pantomime of? Sleights of courtship,
Postures of delight, grief, vanity, idolatry I see

All around me more sharp and subtle for not being
Done in a style. Dancing has social uses,
I know, but so did elemental spears and punches before
They invented tables for eating and conducting
Verbal negotiation (and does hands
Gripping slyly under a table ever happen
In the middle of a fandango?)
Moreover, if the elemental stuff
Of dancing is banal, the ancient, ritual and customary

Panoply of 'the dance' is incredibly peculiar:
Fellows in feathers, or kilts, or puma-skins,
Guys trinkling little bells down there in Hampshire,
Or folding arms over black boots flicking in the
Urals . . . one surely turns away to find somewhere quieter,

Where one needn't be part of a silly circle
Of grins, clapping hands in moronic unison (I once
Took a pocket torch in, to go on reading – *The Listener*,
I believe – all the way through a Gene Kelly musical).

For ostensible moralist reasons, the
Puritans disliked dancing: but they also
Opposed all giving and wearing of jewellery,
In which they may well have been right; so with dancing,
They may also have come at the truth
From a wrong, religious direction. But, down Oxford Street
These days, whatever the mortgage rate, there jogs
In shine or rain an irrelevant group of chanters
Shuffling to the rhythm of tiny cymbals, opposing

Shaven sublimity to the big, crude, selling
Metropolis around; and *dancing*, in sandals, for converts.
They'd like to see everyone join them . . . how unlikely,
I think; and how such unlikelihood shows
That most of us only don or discard our
Finery, to dance, in a fit of social desperation.
I recall that outside the Hammersmith Palais,
There once was an illuminated sign announcing
A group of performers known as THE SANDS OF TIME.

For months, the words, I surmised, were a motto
Of that establishment: a thousand grains shaken
Nightly in that vast box, a thousand softies
Sifting for life-partners as the hours and days
Ticked on in tawdry, implacable rhythms. Yet the
Dancing prospers – telling how many the world leaves
Despoiled of words, of gestures diverse and specific,
Of shades of forehead, or hintings of finger-tips,
Or any more delicate tremor that speaks the whole thing;

And this is the crux. Tides vary, exact shelvings
Of pebbles on shores don't repeat, while patterns of clouds
Are never the same, are never *patterns*. Raindrops,
At unforeseen moments run, and weigh, down, minutely,
A million particular grass-blades: movement, movement,
Everlastingly novel shifts of a universe not
Gracelessly ordered, not presided by a setter of
Regulations. Vanity is so sad pretending to represent
Nature with humans dancing. Those who can move need not dance.

NEGOTIATION

In the same post, the Old Fox receives
Word that he is in overdraft at the bank,
And a gas bill for £3.69.

Ten days later, the Gas Board write again, in red, 'They would
Be grateful if . . .' The Old Fox waits.

Two weeks later, the Gas Board write, in red again, some
Phrases underlined, 'Regret, you do not tender payment within

Seven days, supply disconnected, charge for re-connection.'
The Accounts Officer's signature is stamped below.

Six days later, the Old Fox carefully writes a letter:
'Thank you for, apologies for any inconvenience,
Do not wish cause difficulty, wonder if payment
Of sum outstanding *by instalments*, very grateful, Yours etc.'

A week having passed,
Drinking coffee made on his undisconnected cooker,

The Old Fox reads, 'Must regretfully state, not customary,
Payment by instalments when sum entailed so small,
No alternative but to ask, within five days,
Supply disconnected unless, Dictated by the Accounts Officer
And signed in his absence . . .'

Four days passing, the Old Fox writes, 'Thank you courteous
reply,
Recollect (which is untrue) kindly permitting me
Payment by instalments, previous occasion, some years ago,
Comparable sum, possibly consult your records, appreciate
Your looking into this, regret any delay caused,
Only anxious to settle account as soon as possible.'

The Gas Board writes after a week, ignoring this.
'Supply disconnected unless . . .' The Old Fox rejoins,
'May I direct your kind attention, my letter of,
Possibly held up in the post, possibly crossed with yours of,
Sorry to put you to this, Yours etc.'

'We have looked into our records,' the Gas Board two weeks later,
'Can find no precedent in your case, not our custom with small
amounts,
Must insist on immediate settlement, otherwise steps
Will be taken, supply disconnected, recovery of sum
By legal action, Yours very truly, Accounts Officer'
– Personally signed.

Sadly, then, the Old Fox writes a cheque for £3.69,
Omits (on purpose) to sign it,
And posts it to the Board.

In eight days, the cheque is returned, 'For your signature,
Yours truly.' The Old Fox waits.

A month later, 'We do not appear to have received cheque
On which your signature was requested, bring this
To your kind attention.'

It is winter by now, and the gas fire gleams.
The North Sea roars on the cooker to heat
The Old Fox his supper of Irish stew from a tin.
Lighting his gas water-heater, he runs a bath.
It mellows him. He writes his name at the bottom of the
cheque
(Which will come back 'referred to drawer' in nine days'
time.)
Returning from the pillar box, he picks up the next quarter's
invoice from the mat.

SEVEN OLD MEN ON AN INTER-CITY TRAIN:
A YEATSIAN POEM

The First.   Is that a flood or a lake?
The Second.   I saw a lake.
                And were there flooding there would not be
                                          swans.
The Third.   The swans could have come from a lake, with
                                          all this rain
                A lake could overflow and spawn a flood,
                And cast out swans on it.

The Second.   Yet I look again,
                And see they are not swans but clumps of suds
                Engendered by detergent. Had you but looked
                You would have seen all their necks were under
                                          water.

The Fourth.   But it is unimaginable that suds
               Should drift in wandering pairs as if designed
               To have the look of swans. Now the train has
                                                       passed,
               I speak it with an old man's memory,
               Yet say that nearly all of them were in pairs.

The Second.   Why should not some base tycoon-man, who
                                                       desired
               The pride of an environmentalist,
               Discharge the effluent of his factory
               So that, upon a sudden dreaming glance,
               It looked like swans?

The Fifth.   That would enhance
               A desolate vulgar place, could it but have
               Appearances of companionable swans.

The Sixth.   The poet Yeats loved real swans on real lakes,
               And had a penchant for using them as symbols.

The Third.   And Yeats, I have heard tell, wrote of swans
                                                       on floods.

The Second.   But what would Yeats have thought of clumps
                                                       of suds
               Reclining ceremoniously on a foul scene?
               To forge his symbols would be difficult.
               Yeats was not of an age when factory waste
               Was put on show as swans as a P.R. stunt.

The Fourth.   But Yeats himself was a bit of an old . . . tycoon,
               And symbol swans are just as shadowy
               As foam that moves upon a twilight flood.

The Sixth.   Yet Yeats
          Would not have cried the praise of effluent-swans
          To sanctify some tycoon's greedy till.
          Yeats was –

The Seventh.   I think that Crewe is the
                                        next stop.

A NIGHT IN THE GAZEBO
(1980)

SCARE

I laughed about it afterwards,
But it frightened me at the time.

Yes;
And in entertainment, one axiom is
That scare can be terribly funny:
Those floors that tilt you
Ludicrously here, there, here
In the House of Ghosts;
The wicked fangs on the posters
Dripping hilarious red.

The real worst of horror is
Its shabbiness . . . How nice
If all private scare were awfully
Amusing to retell,
And much better still
If it really, rather wickedly,
Entertained.

– I could hoist my habitual
Skull at its fixed
Mirror in the morning, go at it
Over its shallow covering with
The razor, and receive
Such a comical thrill.

I could open its mouth, gape
Wide with it, make a sound,
And laugh about it afterwards.
It could be a real scream.

A BAD CAT POEM

In the spring of their hope you saw them crouching,
He outside in the sunshine and she inside,
And handling this bad cat back and forth, to and fro
Through the flap. And back through the flap.
They were trying to coax it to work the flap.

That summer the cat was not learning at all,
Though they pushed it persistently, head
First and tail last, towards each other
Through the yielding flap in the humid dark,
She inside, he outside, with fists full of moulted hairs.

And by the autumn still it had not learnt,
While the air was not kindly any more:
The flap on its hinges grated, he outside
Forcing hard the reluctant brute to her inside,
Who received it with aching hands.

It had to be winter next; it would not learn now.
It had never made it once of its own accord:
It had only ever let itself passively
Be jostled to and fro through the grinding hole,
To and fro, back and forth, she inside, he outside,

And both of them getting horribly impatient.

THE INFORMATION

When the Library of Congress is finally
Reducible to a cube one inch by one
Inch by one inch, you are going to need to lose
Absolutely nothing: stored and retrievable

A pear-core once left gangling on an ashtray,
The moment of Amanda's purple scarves touched
Sadly into order, the whole of Le Figaro,
And the accurate timbre of all your departed
Cryings-in-the-night. None of this
Will be vanishing any more.

Up there, instead of shining empty sky
(The still clear sunlight you are walking in
With terrors in your head) will be
A building specially built to set this right:

In any of a thousand rooms it will
Be possible for somebody to remain
For all of life after infancy till death,
Fed and evacuated and re-clothed
In a see-through cubicle, flicking up fact after
Fact and image upon image, actually
Playing his infancy back; working with his keepers
At the reasons, there, for needing to do such a thing.

AN ELEGY ON MADEMOISELLE CLAUDETTE

Mourning the final death from disbelief of one
Who lies now farther out than her rival's sword;
The sea, having had her at last, being
A fit receptacle and outcome. She
Was thirty-two when she died, I having
Given her first credulity when I was eight,

And the ideal reader. Somewhere they met,
Her fatalism, my childhood, and made strange friends:
She held her world with fingertips of ice
On chalices of poison. She was in the eyes

Pulling mine at fifteen over café floors, she stared
Out from trains, she dared in time to come near and be

No different, even when she undressed. The spell didn't
Break, because she was always gone next morning,
A skyline figure on horseback, not leaving a note.
And this continued some while, her cloak
Flowed at numberless parties, and she nurtured
Linguistic codes beyond mine, and had flats

(Which I never went to) all mauve lights and white divans,
Acting indestructible enough to be
A life-force in her way, a fuel for one kind
Of imagination. But what could she keep when
Life coarsened, and truth walked in? Well,
She thrived for a while by updating her devices,

Like – playing the metropolis, all the sleights of
Communications, the trick of the very new:
She was good at sudden taxis, away, in the small hours,
Had a dreadful skill with things like the letter
Never sent because of the promise to phone,
Never kept. And she had this vague gallery of

'Friends' to refer to, in a sensual, significant abstract,
No names vouchsafed. She was trying hard, was desperately
Applying the cosmetics of decline. – But she's
Abstract herself now; finally dead; not
Struck down by some other in contest, not replaced
By odder enchantments, not vanquished by any

Conversion from Snow Queens to Earth Mothers, none
Of that: she just couldn't keep up the pose.
It was not so long back that her last departure
Took place. She put out one entreating hand in velvet,
But it looked like something ghost-written for her.
I tried to feed those plaintive metaphors, I searched

The depths of my compassionate soul for faith
To keep her alive; but all the same she died.
And sad the way daylight lastly saw her sink,
Poor Mademoiselle Claudette: leaving shadows of stances only,
Vague rags of garments, tawdry stage properties,
And terribly dry pink tissues on bedroom floors.

UNION MAN

His liquid lunches will not have unhoned
This lean man, upright at the bar
With the minutes of the last executive
In a thick buff wallet, listening precisely
And working through strategies. His brow
Is furrowed with niceties, his craft
Is the unravelment and intertwining
Of clauses in tense agreements. He gives
A week-end course in grievance and recompense,
And Monday, drives via home to all his high
Cabinets of cases, when the telephone
Clangs to the carpet as he stretches out far to a file
On a distant shelf, and listening precisely.
In a city where minds are slabbed with gold,
He builds a sheltering-wall of brick; and how
The commonwealth doth need such justices.

PROCEDURAL

The Old Fox sits at the front in the Chairman's eye, he
Questions the Apologies for Absence, he
Questions the Minutes, including
The accuracy of the amendments in these Minutes

To the Minutes of the meeting before last, he
Raises Matters Arising for half an hour.

Then he
Carps at the order of items on the Agenda,
Queries the omission of items *from* the Agenda,
Interrupts, interjects, raises Points of Information,
Asks innocent (loaded) questions, has serious Points of Order,
Puts down motions, puts down amendments to motions,
Puts down amendments to amendments, questions the voting,
Wants the Chairman to state again exactly what it is
They have decided by the voting,
Wants his disagreement with the Chairman's decision minuted,
Quotes the Constitution,
Waves the Companies Act.

The Old Fox proposes the creation of
Sub-committees, steering committees, working parties and
Working groups, and declines election
To any of them himself. Any Other Business
Is devoted to matters raised by the Old Fox alone.

When the time to decide the Date of Next Meeting arrives, he
Objects on sound grounds to every possible date.
The desk diaries wearily rise from dispatch cases once again,
The overcoats stay unbuttoned, the great white pages
Turn and flutter and the flutter becomes a wind
And the wind becomes a gale tearing
At the darkness outside the window,
At the darkness in everybody's soul in the steamed-up room.

When the storm subsides, the Old Fox
Has disappeared until the next time.

FROM
COLLECTED POEMS
(1983)

poems not in individual volumes

YOU'LL SEE

They all talked about growing into,
Growing into, growing into.
They said: You will grow into it.

– But it isn't mine,
And it's not for me.
– You will grow into it,
You'll see!

– But it hangs down below my knee,
It is too long for me.
– Oh it will fit you soon,
It will fit you splendidly.

– But I will sulk, and I will say
It is too long, it is no use,
No! I will sulk, and struggle,
And refuse!

– You will grow into it,
And love it,
And besides, we decided
You should have it.

No! – But wait –
Wait a moment . . . Do I see
It growing shorter at the knee?
Is it shrinking gradually?
Is it getting shorter?
Is it getting tighter?
Not loose and straggly,
Not long and baggy,
But neater and brighter,
Comfortable?

Oh now I *do* like it,
Oh now I'll go to the mirror and see
How wonderful it looks on me,
Yes – there – it's ideal!
Yes, its appeal
Will be universal,
And now I curse all
Those impulses which muttered 'Refuse!'
It's really beautiful after all,
I'll wear it today, next week, next year
– No one is going to interfere,
I'll wear it as long as I choose.

And then, much later, when it wears,
And it's ready for dumping under the stairs
When it doesn't actually really fit me
Any longer, then *I'll* pass it down,
I'll give it to someone else
When it doesn't fit me,
And then they'll have it,
They'll *have* to have it,
They'll have to love it,
They'll see, they'll see.

They'll have to grow into it like me!

AN ORCHARD PATH

A guilty tremor in the chime of six
From his dishevelled mantelpiece . . . She waits
For the plaint of the express along the cutting,
Which she guesses the wind will let her hear,
Then she rises, in a calm of strict obedience,

And walks off obediently to be back,
Securely seated in her drawing-room,
As the doors of the carriages gape and slam.

– Though one day the train has left, she is running
And scarcely home before her lawyer husband
Is entering and handing his hat naively
To the discreet old fellow in the hall.
Catching her breath, she comes in from the garden
As if from the garden and nowhere else,
Dividing the curtains no more than her hair
Would be slightly rearranged by an innocent breeze.

– And later still, one day the whistle-call
Dies out, she hears it, over the summer fields,
And she does not move at all. She stands here still,
Though the train is already some way on,
And allocating other destinies.
The lawyer is destined to the empty house.
Her hair is neat. She smiles for the man in this room.
He stares at his prize incredulous and afraid.

FROM HIS CHILDHOOD

Rain, said Nanny, Rain is to test our courage,
Dirt is to test our cleanliness,
Hunger our patience,
And night is to test our fear of darkness.
But rain is to test our courage.

That was because it rained all the time very hard
Where we lived as children,
In the house with the nineteen rooms of forbidden books

(To test how we could conquer the thirst to read)
And a few permitted books in the sitting rooms,
But Nanny in a book-lined room we might never enter,
In a turret above the lawn where the croquet hoops
Were feet deep in water for very much of the time.

But Courage, said Nanny, wellingtons on,
Backs up, chins up, and best foot forward
In a long line, holding tightly on to each other
– Out!

So the small but courageous band of us
Paddled hand-in-hand onwards,
Nanny first, me second,
Then the third and fourth, diminishing in size
To the very smallest who came infallibly last,
Head just above water.

And as we sadly struggled, the small cold hand
Of my youngest brother
Slipped out of the grasp of the one next above him in age.
And when that next one tired, her hand
Released the fingers of the sibling senior to her,
And the line fell gradually apart,
Leaving me
Waving frantically after Nanny, who was far ahead
And had almost disappeared.

But *Courage!*

The call of Nanny rang distantly over
The widening waters in the dark,
And returned in echoes from the other shore.
The waterfowl answered in imitation and unison
To comfort each other

And Nanny's cry merged into theirs,
Growing fainter and fainter in the rain until
It became at last an everyday sound you hear
And think little about for very much of the time.

DOORWAY

Where it stood by the roadside, the frame for a view,
It made the step from one weed-patch to the next
A metaphor. If I chose to walk across
This threshold to a mansion never built,
Could I manage to come back? Having left the road
To stroll into the fields, I saw this lintel
Presenting its challenge. And what it said was, *Walk*

Through this door, you are going to walk through,
After which you will not be the same. I had thought,
Was I always on a journey to that place?
– And now, was I always travelling to where
I am to-night, by a fire toning down to grey
Its image in those glasses, beside the girl
Asleep in the opposite chair? To such a stop?

To-night is six months onwards from that voice
Which said, *You have reached a stage where you must walk through,*
And not expect to return to what you were.
I am here because I turned back from that view,
Shaking my head and smiling, walking on
To where this girl smiles, in apparent sleep,
And stretches.What she does first when she wakes

Is pick the glasses up, they suddenly
Shine scarlet from the curtains. *What were you thinking?*
She says, as she goes past. I shake my head,
And smile, watching the fire. She goes on past
Its dying coil, then I realize she has stopped
And turned at the doorway behind me, tilting
The glasses in her hand. And has said, *Walk through.*

FROM

THE OLD FLEA-PIT

(1987)

LOOKING AT HER

When he looked at her, he invariably felt
Like stretching his arms up, as if about to do
A long and lustrous yawn. Of course she knew
She had that effect; and whether she lounged or knelt,
Or walked or simply stood, he was never clear
If she was prepared and eager to let him bring
His hands down around her neck, and press her near
– Or would shake her head and permit him no such thing.

This was her talent, to stir both lust and doubt,
She did it the best of all feats she was able;
And therefore other women felt sure she bored
The men she attracted; since all of them, without
Her seeming to provoke them, of one accord
Would yawn and thump their fists down on the table.

PROFOUNDEST LOVE

She gave him sand from the Tyrrhenian Sea,
He sent her a present of sand from the shores of Lake Erie.

He dropped some grains of her sand on the edge of the lake,
But kept the others, it helped him remember her.
She mingled a bit of his sand with the verge of the sea,
But retained some grains in a tiny box because
They reminded her of him.

And this was happening everywhere in the world,
Whole deserts exchanged between Asia and Africa,
And people everywhere swopping seedlings and saplings,
Whole forests exchanged between Finland and Brazil.

Cat-lovers transplanted whiskers from their cats:
'My cat has your cat's whisker and yours mine.'
We think of each other much more often that way.

I stood by the motorway watching the sand trucks pass,
I saw huge lorries transporting uprooted trees,
I saw vets' ambulances speeding with mad blue lights
– The whiskers for the transplants.
My name is Vladimir Nikolaich:
Back indoors I switch on a radio I cannot understand,
I am in High Wycombe, the news is in English here.
My Rosemary knows no Russian, I love her so much,
And she is in Kharkov switching on the radio
And comprehending nothing in the least

– Except that we exchanged for one another,
And think of each other very much indeed.
Ours was an act of the profoundest love.

IN JANUARY

In the salt-marshes, under a near black
Sky of storm or twilight, the whole day
Dark on the creeks where the wind drives wavelets back
Against the filling tide, I have lost my way

On a path leading nowhere, my only guide
The light half-way up a television mast
Five miles across the waste; and if I tried,
I could imagine hearing, under this vast

Raw silence of reeds and waters, the deep drone
Of generators, gathering up the power

To send its message out; and, stopped alone
By this channel's edge, revisit a lost hour

At a restaurant table, in a vanished place
(An organ chiming in the hushed cave below)
When three sat smiling in an alcove space
And saw their futures, thirty years ago . . .

And ten years earlier, learn each adverb clause
Written out in the spring by those in dread
Of School Certificate; without much cause
For fearing death as long as they had read

The good green textbooks. Further back, next to me,
Her pencils in a leather pouch, her dress
A blur of gentle yellow, is a she
Who smiles with such a sidelong vividness

I can even touch her hand. And further still,
I walk up between desks rising in tiers,
And see the old imperial pictures fill
The walls of the same room, lit by gasoliers

– My father's now. Then suddenly return
To the path over the marshes, and the light
On the meccano mast, which tries to burn
As strongly as a fixed star, secure and bright

Against the black of nightfall; and provides
Small quizzes for our lounges, puppets that grin
To tame the evening's terrors. England hides
Its head in its small comforts . . . Seeing in

– Alone and lost and darkling – this New Year,
I stare round at the dark miles of this nation,
And through the winter silence only hear
The loveless droning of its generation.

IN A RESTAURANT

The facing mirrors showed two rooms
Which rhymed and balanced beautifully,
So everything we wore and ate
Shone doubly clear for you and me.

In the next image after that
Life seemed the same in every way:
Green bottles and white tablecloths
And cutlery as clean as day;

But in the third, things looked a mite
Less brilliant than in the first two . . .
A sort of mist was falling on
The features of a dwindling view,

And by the time our gaze had gone
Searching down to rooms eight and nine,
The world seemed darker, and confused,
Its outlines harder to define,

Its faces tinier. There, instead
Of warmth and clarity and bright
Colours for everything, we saw
A shadow land, a listless light

Which neither of us understood:
A place so closed and small and black
It nearly hurt, smiling, gripping
Our glasses harder, coming back.

WATERMARK

The lovely Anita, in earrings already
At twelve, in the nineteen-forties, looks out today
Through a Speak Here perspex veil in a Barclay's Bank.
With her awesome self-possession, she was equal
To any approach; and strolled the – respectable – streets
Surrounded by gallants who furnished heavy aid
Against strangers who dared a look at one precious gilt lobe.

Our middle age should have altered a lot of things
– The shy boy level now with the beautiful doll,
One broke and the other plain. But where life's ledger
Builds columns of meticulous disenchantment,
Anita still sits tight at the clasp, making sure
That its cheques and balances add up to a dead stop
On all extravagant longings; a tarnished bell
Calling gallant support against those who might grasp the gold.

BEFORE THE GAME

This is the coin
spinning in air
to decide who wins the toss.

This is the thumb that flicked the coin
spinning in air
to decide who wins the toss.

This is the hand that owns the thumb
that flicked the coin
spinning in air
to decide who wins the toss.

This is the brain that controls the hand
that owns the thumb
that flicked the coin
spinning in air
to decide who wins the toss.

And this, over here, is the twelfth man,
who lent the coin
as a method of being noticed for something
if not for his part in the game.

It is the custom here that the loser of the toss
keeps the coin as a consolation
for the brutality of Fate.

The owner of this coin did not know of the custom,
or he would not have lent for the purpose
a rare doubloon
of the Emperor Paronomasia IV.

As it spins, he watches it, trying to seem unaffected,
thinking, Will I ever get it back?

The situation is complicated by the fact
that the doubloons of the Emperor Paronomasia IV
have two heads.

SCENE FROM THE FIFTIES

The three-year-old who will not go to bed
Tugs Gunga's tail, and Gunga patiently
Permits him to, because he understands.
An animal *knows* when it is children.

Eight o'clock now, in the drawing room
Of a house of proconsular maxims, built
In Hampshire in memory of the hills;
The lights of the town could be any town's.

She can no longer see to write, or hear
To think, so the elderly lady
Turns on the light above the wicker chair,
And licks her letter down, and turns to watch.

Watching her grandchild and the darkening fields,
She thinks, *He knows, he knows*: inside the cat
Is a small child psychotherapist resolving
To stay where he is; it makes things easier.

The mould of things seems perfectly secure:
The animals can tell when it is men;
The old man in the bedroom winds up the clock
Which tells him what time it is in Simla;

The daughter in the kitchen daintily
Prepares an England to receive them all;
The pile of 45s in Mary's room
Is not seen as something doing any harm.

THE RAIN DIARY

For my geography project I would keep a rain diary, a record starting on 1st January of the days that year when it rained and approximately how much.

On 1st January there was no rain. On 2nd January there was no rain. It did not rain on 3rd or 4th either. Would I go back to school on 8th January with nothing to show? Only blank pages with the dates in blueblack italic and the expectation of punishment?

Amanda kept a sunshine diary. The sun shone all the time that New Year, every day was like the legendary 1st January 1942. I saw long shadows of bare trees in Amanda's garden revolving on the stiff white grass as the sun crawled low and bright round the Warwickshire sky. Amanda, day by day, logged her hours of sunshine in duffle coat and mittens, putting out her tongue to warm her finger tips.

Tiny planes inched over the blue from the aerodrome leaving lacy strips of vapour which crumbled into strung-out blurs. There was no rain on 5th, 6th or 7th. I gained a sense of what life in general would be like.

On 8th January I stood at 8.55 a.m. on the worn stone step of the school with my blank diary – and raindrops fell. But I had no time to write anything down, the bell was pounding in the school campanile and we could not be late. So I opened my rain diary and let the rain fall into it, stain it and crinkle it, as the others fled past me into school.

To which rain I added my own joyful tears, knowing that Amanda might have statistics but I had a concrete event.

A FEAR OF WILDERNESS

They leap without letting on they intend to,
These cats. Assuming they always do land
In amenable safety, they cling to
Your lap with four paws cold from the darkness.
You shiver at the ice they bring in them.

But slowly your legs regain a heat,
Their claws retract, and the vacillating tail
Has finished; the four feet now turning warm.
What had been once, outside the door, a fear
Of wilderness is now a comfortable

Interesting glow, of cities seen from trains
You are neither entering nor pausing in.
You pat and patronize, they settle down
To a steady breathing. In the yellowed light
The two of you are rational animals.

MARES

The pink dog darts about on the edge of the sideboard.
The water rises eagerly to his feet.
It will fill the polished horn of the gramophone,
Submerging the strings of the salon orchestra
In their antique love song. The tenor is singing, 'Turn
The garden tap off, love, poor Spot will drown.'

Commander of a pirate underground train,
A prominent liberal journalist guides it
Up the tunnel. In the illumined coaches,
The passengers undress for hard-porn video
And electro-convulsions. On an escalator,
An inspector points and shouts, 'We'll get you, you bastard!'

Nothing wrong with the great capacious bed,
Or with the three schoolgirls all snuggling up;
And no jealousy of the smallest one, with glasses,
When I see her next morning by the fruit machine;
She is only cutting a loose thread off the sweater
Of a Pakistani nuclear physicist.

If I went a day earlier than I plan to,
They wouldn't shoot me on the hotel steps;
If I arranged another hotel altogether,

Or took an earlier flight, they still might not;
If I went by sea, not air, that might be safer.
All the hotels are my former Oxford college.

Petronella sidles up smiling to tell me
How the old flea-pit has suddenly re-opened,
A stone's throw from the crematorium.
We ought to queue early, I like Petronella,
Her lips are flecked with urticaria,
They love her at the crematorium.

A fabulous welcome: met at the station
By an orchestra of centaurs in dinner jackets.
'We'd like to give you the honour' – the first violin –
'Of conducting us in some items.' 'But I've never –'
'Oh yes you have!' – 'But I'm unable –' 'Please,
Here's the baton. You know *La Boutique Fantasque*.'

The woman has been working hard on relaxation
In front of the cameras. Against all custom,
She lights and draws on a black and white cigarette.
The smoke through her teeth fills up, blanks out, the screen.
We only hear an antique voice, proclaiming.
The water rises eagerly to her feet.

POLITICS

Lighting the cigarettes I need not have smoked,
I almost burnt my beard; but also found
My eyes went squinting down towards the flame,
And the page, or face, or room on the farther side
Slid out of focus into broken halves.
That was my fault entirely; but is it mine

If that girl with the Abbey National plastic bag
Is standing there, on a strip of grass between
Dual carriageways? She is ruining
My focus of this scene as a unified
View of pollution where, on the farther side,
One car in two is a speeding panda
With its blue nipple flashing to smash the pickets.

I fix my attention on the alarming Law:
The girl is on its side by standing there;
She puts an unconscious flaw and distraction
In front of my perceptions – am I to blame
If she's rather too attractive for the view?
Old men may want their youth back, but old nations
Pine for the liberties of middle-age,
The mortgage paid off, the authority . . .
In Baker Street, Sherlock Holmes smoked a pipe,
Which keeps the flame much farther from the face.
Will someone please guide that girl to safety
And clear my field of vision, before the smoke
Rolls down my throat and blinds the eyes with fears?

FROM
THE OBSERVATION CAR
(1990)

SEA PICTURES

1

A man is bicycling along the sands,
Predicting the firm stretches where his wheels
Will not sink down; he listens to their hiss
As all the waves of the sea push towards him
In amenable ripples. He rode here down a lane
Where September offered all colours of blackberry
At the same time; at the dunes he lifted up
His vehicle over the gorse; and on the beach,
He set it down and pedalled off westwards.
He notices the boat far out, its windows,
Its smoke, and the man and woman on the sundeck.
When the boy turned and lashed out with his spade

2

At his aggravating sister, what could they do
But condemn him to stay and guard the clothes?
So the rest of the family, sister included,
Who would, in the boy's opinion, not have suffered
The same indignity had she swung the spade,
Make tracks towards the distant recession of waters,
Ignoring the tears which are flooding down over
His abolished castle. And then, double spy, Sod's Law,
He is stung by a wasp, and his older brother
Has to sprint back and see why he is roaring.
He comforts him; and picks up his dropped spade.
There was once a woman absolutely averse

3

To having her name romantically inscribed
On the sands, it was better to have it called
Romantically over the waters. And this dread
Of having even the letters of that word
Dispersed by the tide was one of her variants
Of the fear of death. But the elder of the two boys
Hasn't heard of such reluctance, he takes the spade
The smaller one is bored with, seeing it builds
No castles by itself, and begins to write
Some initials on a wide, firm, yellow stretch
Twenty yards or so away from the family clothes.
'The broughams of legitimate love' which the classic

4

Novelist saw, are out this afternoon,
Creatures of slow and polished habit, getting
The best of the warmth of mid-September where
A line of them has poised itself sedately
Along the clifftop, windscreens to the sun
Which glints as well on countless points far out
On the surface of the not-too-restless sea,
Towards which in the distance a family
Of discontented people slowly treks.
At rightangles to them, behind them, a man
Will cross in one hour's time on a bicycle.
Two grandparents from one brougham see the two boys

5

As they gaze down from a clifftop rail the Council
Is still allowed to paint; and notice too
The boat almost stationary in the water

Half-way up to the horizon, though they can't see
The man still on the sundeck. In their boot
Are the blackberries taken from where they parked
In a safe straight lane, turned on their hazard lights,
Went round and checked the handles of every door,
And picked with plastic bags along the hedges,
While the dog sat mutely up in its barred-off space
And imagined human reasons for doing this.
In a cabin of the ferry, the woman lets

6

The door close behind her, having come back down
From the sundeck leaving the man; and she gives
This worried frown to herself in the mirror,
And goes hard at the problem of her hair,
All fraught and fixed and clenched by the attentions
Of only a slight breeze, with a honey-coloured
Comb. It needs to be coaxed, she needs to be coaxed,
But the engine beat is steady, the sea quiet,
And she balances easily. She is happy
With the spray that rinses her window, and decides
To take the camera with her when she goes.
'They are unloading coal at that small seaport

7

'Exactly – there!' The man has entered, starting
An uneasy conversation, and they both look
Through the window at an old tub releasing
An irregular cargo of brownish stuff
In rumbling slopes and screes as it creaks and stirs
In the harbour waters; holidaymakers watch.
'They say that coal has come from India,'

Unloading in the profound September sun
Which day by day seems more impervious
To the onset of autumn, as the woman's hair
Seems impervious to the corrections of her comb.
A sign made of coloured bulbs is saying 'Arnold's'. . .

OBSERVATION CAR

At last they arranged it so that you just couldn't see
Out of any train window. You had to focus
On the back of the seat in front, or on the floor,
Or on the obligatory food, wheeled up on trolleys
To where they had strapped you in; though a favoured few
Could end up riding at the rear of the train
In the Observation Car, from where the receding lines
Added ever-increasing length to the two sides
Of an angle wedging acutely into the past.
How fast that terrain seemed, and interesting,
Though it vanished before you guessed it had ever been:
You saw your bridges after you had crossed them,
You learned what was before you saw it coming,
And everyone pointed and said, 'The amazing things
We were missing all that time! If we had known,
We might have stopped the train and got out to enjoy them.'
– In this assuming they were better off
Than the others, sitting boxed in their airline seats
And observing nothing. When occasionally
Someone tried to complain to the guardian who came
Down the gangway cancelling tickets, he would say,
'You are fortunate to have seats, either there or here,
In the midst of such a good metaphor for life.'

ALL BEST

I go with the grain of foreign courtesies
By writing, to somebody met only twice,
I remain, your impassioned eternal lover
Or *My soul is yours each minute of day and night.*
Inevitably, a laughing answer comes:
'No, no! It is all wrong. I tell you, please,
The words we are using here, and you will find
The nearest words in English to say it right.'

So for months all my letters begin and end
With ever more misjudged felicities,
Still striving to please correspondents for whom
I love you until death is no stronger than
Good morning, and for whom not to say,
In concluding the simplest thank-you letter,
I touch you all over, always, in my thoughts
Is tantamount to insult. It does not work.

I watch the leaves turn colour, at different speeds,
And start another letter wondering
Should I go back to intriguing understatement?
The kind I used once, coaxing long threads of hair
From between a pillow and the incomparable
Shoulders which trapped them, so as to release
A head and lips for a more than thank-you kiss
– When I only had strength enough for *kind regards?*

APRIL LIGHT

Slowly the tree falls, and we lean back
On our axes watching it, in the film,
Leaning on arm-rests in the Odeon.
The trunk and riven stump will kill nobody
In the good April daylight we had then.
So when the man with the name my friend had
Thirty years ago, and a credible address,
Dies today in the *Guardian*, struck by a falling tree,
This is fiction, it can't *be* him, it's a common name,
And trees fall commonly in reported storms.
So I don't go to the telephone, and I don't start
To write at last the letter I never wrote
When neglect was slowly cutting away at friendship.
I laugh at the idea, at the superstition,
And lean back in my chair, watching the light
Fall on a spring day killingly like winter.

A DREAM OF LAUNCESTON
(*for Charles Causley*)

So clear and safe and small,
on the nearest horn of
about twenty-seven

steady-breathing fellows
who have me cornered in
a field in North Cornwall

with their overbearing
friendliness (is it that?)
the ladybird allows

a petticoat of wing
and then recovers it.
And then: one pink-and-blue

nose lifts, and a deep note
rides out over the grass
to tremble the yellows

of the low primroses . . .
And 'Shoo' I say, and 'Shoo!'
in my nine-year-old voice

each time the dream comes back.
They do not shoo, and I
will not grow up, at all.

Reading the numbers on
the twitching ears as if
nothing more happened next,

I crave the freedom of
that tiny elegance
to flaunt itself, and fly.

SECRETS FROM AND WITH

'Whirlpool closed for repairs'

At least we were seasick among friends

He who controls the photocopier controls the polytechnic

Religious Hats (a cigarette card series)

Amuse yourself sandpapering the new cathedral

Like musical chairs but adding a new chair every time
        the phonograph stops

Terminal, man. Your data stop here

Did you see that prostitute in a helmet going past
        the window?

The cows are chewing clockwise so we *must* be in the
        northern hemisphere

Can you tell me who lost the losers' race?

Moments of Hideous Indiscretion (a cigarette card series)

He was *disgusting*, Marie Lloyd said he was *disgusting*

And rose again on the third day the organ of the
        Granada Tooting

You've changed, you talk in noun clauses all the time

The last moral maxim going out of the other ear

Grow your beard up to your nose, pull your hat down over
        your eyes, shut your mouth and abstain as if
            you were voting

Are you a Gentleman, or a Player? – I am a Quantity
        Surveyor

Varieties of Post-coital Triste (a cigarette card series)

If you are on your death-bed, why are you doing a handstand?
        – To see the answer printed upside down.

THE AUTOMATIC DAYS

Oral Contact with a Duck

Rise up a brief metal escalator, see
Mrs Gurnard dash into a cubicle,
And dab some powder on her face, and touch
A spot not there this morning, and snatch her bag,
And lift her coat from an alcove and hurry out
Through the suddenly dropping swathe of heat
At the glass doors opening onto the Precinct,
Where, among the concrete pots of late summer flowers,
Goodbody's have put some lime-green litter-bins:
'A Message from Goodbody's: KEEP OUR PRECINCT TIDY!'
– At entirely their own expense. Mrs Gurnard
Drops into one a wrapper from a mint,

And then she goes on with her sandwiches,
And enters the Park by an almost unknown gate,
A small pedestrian gate too narrow
For cars or even horses, used by few,
Where she does not pause to read, on a notice board,
The Regulations, giving opening times
And things not allowed in the Park: no dropping
Of litter, no giving of political speeches,
No playing of musical instruments, no groups
Of more than six persons to play any game
Except on the authorised pitches. She is alone
On this cloudy lunch hour, free of the Summer Skirts,

And a duck walks up towards her, hopefully,
With the arcane, superior look of a species
Not often spotted in the Park, a fowl
Flown in from somewhere else and followed by
A mate in a plumage not to be described
Without a bird book. She undoes her coat,

And the duck appears to scrutinise the disc
She is wearing under it, with her name and role
Punched out in capitals. She calls, and stretches,
And holds out a piece of torn-off buttered crust
To the duck, which stands and . . . stands and . . . Mrs
                                                    Gurnard
Speculates, 'Can you sniff if you have a beak?'

As the duck stands pondering, and Mrs Gurnard
Speaks to it quietly, trying it with the bread,
She seems to sense a moment of inanition,
A second of being mesmerised to nothing . . .
Her stare, as she stares, middle-aged, at the bird
Is like the preoccupation of a child,
Or the acquiescence of senility
In things coming harmlessly close to hand:
A somewhat low point of human consciousness,
A chilly moment when being alive (for her)
Is only being alive to focus clearly
The sniffing beak, and eye, of a strange duck.

The Last of Autumn

On a slack Monday morning (in her dream)
Mrs Gurnard comes in and sees a customer
Paying coins into Tamsin's outstretched fingers.
Tamsin's fingers turn them over onto her palm,
And they transform into toads. Not only that,
But the customer is wearing the Manager's hat
With a square blue disc on it: BEAT THE XMAS RUSH,
And is some peculiar kind of reptile.
Tamsin is also stroking him, or it.
'You are not supposed to stroke a customer,'
She tells Tamsin. Tamsin makes a sign.
Trevor and Beverley only stand and laugh.

On a slack Monday morning, Mrs Gurnard,
Having had a 'frightful night', comes in and sees,
And focuses, only the rain dribbling down
On the windows; she thinks every droplet carries,
Like a shell on its downward racing back,
A small aborted Precinct. And all around,
Xmas is starting up: this year's diaries
(Cheaper since March, and August) all replaced
By next year's; near the typewriters, new shelves
Of gift-packed stationery in pastel boxes;
Mistletoe wrappers round adhesive tape;
Small snowman price tags added to Artist's Pads.

In the Snow

November: Tamsin, helping to window-dress,
Lifts a large cardboard Santa Claus into a window,
A two-dimensional figure of a barelegged
blonde in Santa's red hood and gown,
The traditional elderly bringer of gifts
Updated to please an age not given
To reverence for age, but certain to esteem
The gift of sex. She rides a little sleigh,
And she'll be down your flue in a week or two.
Anyone passing might be forgiven
For doing a double-take thinking she was real.
'Her legs must get cold, in the snow like that!'

The reindeer pulling her could not be real,
But the plainclothes Security at Xmas are.
'You need them then more than any other time,'
Says Mrs Gurnard, quoting the Manager.
They go round in the guise of men-in-the-street,
In fur-collared coats, or jeans and anoraks,
Choosing their gifts with young Security wives.

They examine three-piece suites, watch demonstrations,
And ask about the price of foreign soaps
On the cosmetics. They watch the assistants
Most carefully when they go home at Xmas,
Hands deep in pockets clutching children's shoes.

In the Tinsel

Now it's the time for carols, carols, carols,
Incessantly resounding on the PA,
Only pausing to notify lost children
Taken howling to the playroom and left to swim
In seas of coloured balls. Half of the screens
Show Xmas videos of Seasonal Offers;
Snow is falling in them. A tiger walks
To and fro on his hindlegs the length of the Ground Floor,
And draws attention to the Toys Department
With a sandwich board concealing his lack
Of credible features. Mrs Gurnard turns
A young tramp, sleeping, out of the photo booth,

And Tamsin is in the tinsel. In her dream,
She has stolen it from the Interest Rates display
In the Building Society Xmas window,
And draped it round and round her as she walks
Glittering, as she glides, up the Precinct
Like a distraught one of the recent dead
Who make their way half-dazed through the studio
Mists of the hereafter in a film about
People from a wrecked airship touching down
(So they come to learn) in heaven. And Tamsin is
The youngest one, who never should have died.
It's right her boyfriend joins her at the end.

FROM
IN THE CRUEL ARCADE
(1994)

THE LAST STONE

Moving from hope to hope like stepping-stones,
One day the eyes and feet discovered
That the next step was too huge, they'd reached the last
Stone possible to reach and would stand there always,
Exhausted by that very last lunge forward
Onto its narrow, dry security;
And there would be nothing left to do, but stand
With your shoes having, so far, kept out all the water;
But with your expensive threadbare trousers threaded
By a rising wind, and your little jacket round you
Not enough to keep the cold out; and try, and try,
To hope, to *hope*, you could retain your balance;
This being only half-way across the river . . .

A CORRIDOR

      Several layers of paint never did
Turn the wall in the scullery the matching
Deep green Dad wanted, in the end
It was always pale and peculiar again.
One night there was a hole leading through to a space
Going on and on like the one in the hospital,
With the endless shelves I was told I came from.
On better nights it became the carpeted
Avenue in the basement of the store
Past the springy double beds and the sofas,
And ended where it narrowed between mirrors
Hung both sides head-high down a dimmer stretch
Where people turned their heads all the way along.
I followed it, it changed to an arcade
With tatty lawn-strips of an artificial

Deep green grass. At a counter we stood around,
With a kind of cruel and watchful aunt in charge,
The ping pong balls sprayed up in different colours
From out of a fountain, looking something like
The constituent planets in a diagram
Of the unsplit atom. They dropped if you were lucky
To end up in the small nets you presented
On the ends of bamboo sticks, nets made
Of a tearable fabric like an Xmas
Stocking in a shop, or a big girl's stocking:
You won a money prize for six balls safely
Caught in your net. I would stand for half-an-hour
Or as long as my pennies lasted, but I lost
My money in the end. I always finished
With my net nearly empty, and the woman sent me
Away from her counter to a deep green wall,
Or not a wall, a hole or door which opened
Onto a corridor like the hospital's,
The endless one with all the endless shelves
Where I, they told me whenever I asked,
Had been a dot slowly growing a long long time.

INERTIA REEL

Waking after the nightmare of a too-high urinal

Dawn: a new day waiting, terrified, to be auditioned

I shave, forgetting I have a beard. I dress, not remembering I
meant to slop around in pyjamas. I have a super ego, but is its
memory going?

First Steps in Hypochondria (a Correspondence Course)

Ah, a brisk morning walk! Feeling good, but a bit like a newly-sharpened pencil: a little less left than yesterday

And no real appetite for lunch. I'm offered another nymphet but I'm full up already

Hypochondria Lesson Three: not the strength in your fourth toe you had at forty

Eat All You Want and Still Look Anorexic (a Correspondence Course)

So the afternoon stretches insensibly on, past the hour of my birth in a climatic and economic depression

And tea-time already! Not ready for it, nostalgic about lunch, the oil-cloth on the table, the glass cruet won at hoop-la, the savoury mince

In the newspaper: Barnacles make trusty pets

Hypochondria Lesson Eight: Never stir weak tea, let your toast cool a little, always boil lettuce before eating

Sunset: rehearsal for what might just come right to-morrow evening

Send for your barnacle today (meaning: Pay us to unload our vagrant crustacea on you)

How to relate to your bedclothes (a Correspondence Course)

In the newspaper: Scientists have proved that the time we spend asleep thinking we are awake and the time awake thinking we are asleep cancel each other out

Last thought at night before sleep overcomes my dread of it: Oh, I shall survive; but it will take a second lifetime

INCIDENT IN 1912

The boy, an only child, is taken out
To tea with some cousins. They are a family
Of five exuberant girls; and they dance and shout
In the absolute conviction that you are better
For being five than if you are merely one.
To be a singleton can't be much fun,
So the five of them dance round him mockingly;
And in forty years' time all six receive a letter.

Forty years later, somebody will write
With news for all of these people; but that can wait.
The boy wears a brand-new sailor-suit, the spite
Of the five capering cousins is taken out
On its trim blue smartness: one of them dips a spoon
In the gooseberry jam-pot, and very soon
His trousers are smeared with pips, and a huge great
Blob runs down his collar, all this without

Any protest from their mother, the boy's aunt,
Who is used to such behaviour in her brood
(How can you punish every jape and taunt?)
But upright on the upright piano stands
A sepia photograph of Aunt Caroline,
Indomitable, single and fifty-nine,
Who knows how these girls will not come to much good,
And that the devil finds work for idle hands.

In minutes the boy is close to resentful tears,
He retreats into a corner, the girls pursue;
Aunt Caroline lives on for forty years,
Or, to be precise, she dies at ninety-six.
His parents are enraged, but his mother won't
Presume or dare to utter the word *Don't*
To her sister's children. Aunt Caroline, too,
Would simply watch and ponder these bullying tricks

If she were there. Back home, the stricken boy
Vows never to go back, never to speak, at all,
To these cousins, who so thoroughly enjoy
Being five in the family that they must ridicule
Less fortunate children. Aunt Caroline is poor,
And thrifty; and behind her bedroom door
Has a mirror, fitted loosely to the wall,
Where she stores unspent pound notes. The space is full

By the time she dies, she has had few bills to pay,
So the sum went on increasing. Other hands
Came to count it in the end, hands that knew the way
The law must apportion each intestate pound;
And eventually the solicitor's tidings drop
Onto various family doormats. At the top
The letter says: *In re Miss Caroline Sands,*
Deceased: We beg to inform you we have found

The estate of the above to be valued, net,
At two thousand pounds, most of it cash concealed
At 94, The Crescent. If you kindly let
Us know the names of those to receive due shares
We should be much obliged. The angry boy
Is a married man today; and he learns with joy
The import of this letter, which has revealed
A most amazing justice; and who cares

That he was mocked, nearly forty years ago,
By that spiteful mob for being an only child!
Each branch of this cousinhood will soon know
What share of the two thousand to expect,
And in one large and noisy family,
When they see that the cash will be shared out equally
Between branches, not individuals, a wild
Delight will change to curses. 'Is this a fact,'

One girl exclaims, 'that because I am one of five,
I receive only sixty pounds of this hidden hoard,
While in the post for that one child will arrive
A letter and a cheque for over three
Hundred quid? It isn't fair, it's a disgrace!
That stupid boy, with green jam on his face,
Will be getting five times my share? This is absurd.
We'll write to this solicitor instantly . . .'

But next day she 'phones the boy, to say that she'd
Love to see him, with her sisters, to celebrate . . .

*   *   *

The boy remembers the last time, and is afraid.
Their mockery still hurts him, and the lack
Of kindness in people. Still . . .
                                Though he made that vow

Not to visit them ever again, well *now*
– *No!* He cannot change his mind. It's much too late.
They are planning some strange revenge . . . He will not go back.

NEGLECTED FIRE

My mother says, *That bonfire's still alight,*
But I can't tell where she's pointing. *On the right,*
Can't you see it now?
                        And then I catch one spark
At the far end by the plane tree, in a dark
Recess of the undertrimmed garden where
She does sometimes light fires. So I lean and stare
Through the room the light paints on the window pane

As she holds back the lace curtain, and some rain
– Or sleet, or snow – blurs the garden with sharp spots
Drumming down on the glass. And I shift some pots
On the unsteady scullery table, hoping for
A clearer view as she moves off through the door:
I can't have raked it over properly,
She murmurs guiltily; to herself not me.

But though they went on creeping back into
Our after-supper talk in the room we knew
As 'the kitchen', no one ever thought to go
And make the fires safe; our pre-war radio
Detained us, with its post-war comedies.
While out there in the garden, under the trees,
The flames were obstinately burning on,
My mother was reminding us that one
Small spark could fire a city, she had no doubt
That someone should have gone and stamped them out;
And all loose ends were living wires, they'd kill
If you forgot, and touched them.
                                    But with no will
To act herself she left us reassured
That most fires died out of their own accord.

TWO PROSPECTS OF ADOLESCENCE

(i)
My shoes left neatly side by side alone,
My socks peeled down and draped over a rock,
My trousers rolled in even folds, each fold
(As I was always taught it ought to be)
The exact breadth of a turn-up . . .

I kept them all in sight from the shoreline,
Where I steadied myself on the sand's hard corrugations
And confronted the North Sea with my book.
The wind felt at my feet and at my shin-hairs
As I waited for the sea to catch me up . . .

And I stood it out in ankle-deep ripples, reading
Of the party that echoed in Auerbach's cellar,
And Gretchen growing in the dreams of Faust;
While my friends, up in the dunes, trembled in trances
That dared the flagrance of lovers in Pompeii . . .

(ii)
I am remembering by re-reading you:
We are dancing together over my diary's page,
And we are dangerously breakable!
Oh we would shatter into ruins if
We went any closer, the polite and maladroit boy
And the circling girl . . .
                It's late, I close the book
On my squandering of all that innocence.
How it could have prepared me . . .Why did I never see
That the fear and inexperience provided
Premonitions of a truth it took so much
More living to recognise: all there ever was
Was breaking?
            I am longing in the dark
To recover the feel of those intact gyrations,
Your fingers resting on my shoulder and scarcely
Touching it, my right hand at your waist,
My left hand neat in your clammy and clean hand.

A WALK BY MOONLIGHT

I cross the side of the Square at a safe walk,
And shall soon be passing the solitary guard
At the Palace. Up beyond him, one in a dark
Leather jacket stands; and waits. I am assured
By his noncommittal look that I have been seen.
This is ten seconds after nine-thirteen.

Keeping to one of the two permitted routes,
I am thirty yards from where he leans on the tall
Palace railings, when he devalues his cigarettes
By lighting one. TRAIASCA PARTIDUL
COMUNIST ROMAN, say the letters of the sign
On the Central Committee, opposite. Two lights shine

From its huge grey rectangle. One is a bright
Slant of yellow from the door, which strangely stands
Wide open, and the second is a late
Lamp lit in a fourth-storey window, a light which sends
The message that Someone is working up there,
At nine-fifteen above Republic Square!

And are they suspicious of me, walking up
The pavement towards them? Because the man
Now approaches the soldier (whose trained grip
Doesn't slacken for a second on his gun). . .
Could it be that I become the subject of
The muttered conversation these two have?

Now I've passed, but their faces are still watching the only one
To disturb them for some while; and though their voices
Talk freely, they still talk quietly. When I look in
-to the clockmakers' window I see other faces
Saying it's nine-sixteen and all is well.
I'm two minutes away from the hotel.

*   *   *

Now that I'm back I have enjoyed my outing.
The clerk at the desk is ready with my key.
When I enter the lift, which has been waiting
While I've been out, I get its night and day
Rattle of muzak; and I hope the door
Will open, at the hush of the fourth floor.

Yes, my shirt hangs on the mirror, where it was,
And my notepad hasn't moved. On the counterpane
Are my dictionary and tablets.
                          I'll watch the news
With *Telejurnal*; after which the screen
Will give me the Inspector, the good Roman,
To-night, and no doubt for some nights to come. . .

*   *   *

If anyone is listening, I'm at home.

Bucharest 1987

IN MOSLODINA

'If we never learn much from history it is because
"we" are always different people.'

In the Tourist Hotel somebody leaves a tap
Running too long. The first drip to fall on me
Strikes at my left thigh; the second stays
Poised over the armchair, then suddenly
Runs, and drops several inches farther up;
The third and fourth I catch in two ashtrays.

Forgetting my own bath, I rush to get
Dressed and raise Cain, cursing a world with too
Many forgetful fools in it, and surely far
More than there used to be? Plus, a huge new
Tribe of the unknowing, happy to let
Some others tell them what their memories are.

The drips fill tumblers, vases. Through the dead
Door of the room upstairs a national song
Booms to drown my knocking. Girls in folkloric dress
Light candles on T.V. . . . . I watch a long
Dark, cross-shaped patch on the ceiling form, and spread:
A continent of sheer forgetfulness.

BASTARD

Into a suddenly sunny spring dawn
A bastard creeps out through a crack in some
Until-then immaculate-looking woodwork.

He inhales the air and smiles, and everything
Looks good to him. And so he takes a few
Experimental paces, trying out

His legs and wondering what clothes to wear:
A city suit? Some jeans and a baseball cap?
Or an 'I ❤ my building society' T-shirt?

Because he plans to walk into an Organisation,
To stir things up inside an Organisation.
He is going to Go For It and get others Going,

And he's past Reception already, and up
In an express lift to a penthouse suite already,
And they have an office waiting for him already,

And his first dictated letters on a screen.
In the other offices, behind their hands,
They are talking about him, quite a lot,

They are saying, 'How did that bastard get that job?
I'd like to know where the hell he came from!
I'd like to see his qualifications for doing

What he does.' – All talk, and he knows it, it's safer
To talk than to act, the smaller bastards
Know the truth of that from long experience,

They've learnt to carry on and keep their heads down
To protect their own bit of woodwork.
                                        So all goes well,
With the faxes slithering out from other bastards

In other penthouse suites all round the world,
And the graph turning upwards on the wall-chart in
The Bastard's Conference Room, the spread-sheets glowing

With the marvellous figures the Bastard envisages;
And his desk is clear and shiny, and people's smiles
Are amiable and innocent, or seem so.

Or seem so . . . In his deep suspicious brain
The Bastard worries occasionally that their lips
May be smiling, smiling for him, but not their eyes.

Still, for now, things go splendidly, the Bastard is seen
On 'State of the Art' and 'Man of the Week', and has
A 'Room of my Own' and a 'Holiday of my Choice'.

– And then one day a casual conversation
Stops short when he enters a room without warning
And another day the people do not stop

When he comes round the door, but self-consciously keep talking
With knowing looks, and ever-widening smiles.
The Bastard pretends he hasn't noticed, but

He goes back to his office and he thinks
'Those bastards could be ganging up on me . . .
I must watch that little bastard with the haircut.'

The Bastard is full of fear and fantasy,
And the fantasy that made his world for him
Becomes a fantastic fear of losing it:

His mirror tells him always to guard his flanks,
And never leave his knife-drawer open when
He turns his back on even his secretary

– But he does have courage. It tells him to have it out
Face-to-face with his team of Assistant Bastards
And find out what the hell is going on.

Oh no, they'll never tell him half the story,
Oh yes, they'll sit and talk behind their hands,
But he can still fire the lot; or he thinks he can.

Today they are gathered round a table, with vellum pads
Which some of them are writing or doodling on,
And some are self-confidently leaving quite untouched.

It's the ones who pick up no pencils and take no
Notes who are the most dangerous. They know
The result they want without fidgeting about it;

Especially the little bastard with the haircut.
He speaks in code but it's clear what he's implying:
The Bastard is letting the Organisation down,

It ought to do better; and all the smallest bastards,
The shareholders' democracy, have been stirred
To demand a different bastard at the top.

This year they're eager for a different scene,
This year they're after a man with a different style,
This year they'd like a bastard with a haircut.

The Bastard's hand is turning clammy on
His thoroughly doodled vellum pad,
The sky is blue for other bastards now.

He sees what is coming next, and he'll speak out first.
He rises from the table, he looks at them
With steady eyes, and steady eyes look back,

Though the lips are smiling. 'I've seen your game!' he shouts,
'I've sussed it out – you're just a lot of *bastards*,
A lot of dirty, crooked, scheming *bastards!*'

When the door slams hard behind him they look at each other
And shake their heads with humane and pitying smiles.
'Poor bastard,' one compassionately murmurs.

The haircut says, 'It wasn't easy, but
It had to be.' And a third: 'I'm so relieved
It's over and we can breathe.' And a grinning fourth

In a flak jacket moves into the Bastard's chair
As the sun sets golden, and the immaculate walls
Begin to look like very porous woodwork.

BALLAD FORM AGAIN

Seated one day in the sauna,
    Hands on my steaming knees,
Counted my two feet, got it right,
    Thought,What do I do with these?

Numbered my human failings,
    Pardoned them one by one,
Took a shower and dried myself,
    Walked out into the sun

– Snatched for my dark, dark glasses
    Moment I hit the light;
Find shade a little easier,
    Can't take the world too bright.

Strolled through the City Centre,
    Followed the One Way signs
To the Consumer Precinct,
    Saw the new clothes designs,

Saw the new architecture
    In the new eclectic style:
Post-modern Bauhaus Gothic.
    Looked at the gargoyles smil-

Ing on the old church pinnacles
    As the sky turned grey then black,
Folded my dark, dark glasses,
    Thought of turning back

But pressed on, with my umbrella,
    As the hail began to pelt:
More climatic experience
    Under my belt . . .

For shelter, was there a tea-room
    Or a library to be found?
No – only the hypermarkets
    Gleaming all around.

Trod carelessly in the gutter,
    Water gushed over me;
Thought, Forces of Nature as usual,
    Behaving amorally.

My feet being wet in my footwear,
    I decided to call it quits,
So I lowered my umbrella,
    Collected my few wits,

And checked the number of gargoyles
    – Thirteen vindictive elves!
Thought, Don't take the piss out of gargoyles,
    They do it for themselves.

Headed back home, determined
    Not to go out again
To waste the good of a sauna
    Walking in lousy rain.

Thought, Shoes which let in water
    Should be junked for sterner stuff;
And the same goes for the ballad form:
    Enough is enough.

THE CAT WITHOUT EMAIL
(2001)

POEM ABOUT MEN

Thing about girls was, they were everywhere!
They lived above furniture shops, alighted on
Your field of vision in recreation grounds,
And licked ice-creams by corner-shop entrances,
And sat in groups in the very same seats each day
Of the first bus home the moment school came out.
They could be the daughters of plumbers, or officers
In local government, or sit two rows in front
In the Regal, and you'd never seen *them* before.
There could be girl cousins with them, or friends who'd come
From a distant town, and you thought, *Please don't go back!*

Women are different, though, living with local
Government officers, married to plumbers, leaving
Cars on rainy superstore parking places,
With hardened furrows set in their twenty
-Nine year old faces; complicit in mortgages,
With futures on too-fragile salary scales.
I believe that women have never been girls at all,
Just women from the start, kept somewhere else
When the streets were full of girls from everywhere
– And finally released to do away
With girls for their lack of brutal obviousness,
Girls for their courage in being unusual,
Girls for their cheek in being their younger selves.

THREE 'O' POEMS

1. *A Defence of Reading*

O in the spring the legs were out,
    And they were smooth and trim,
And every eye that saw them felt
    They must be out for him.

O in the spring the legs were out,
    And they were cold and pure,
And chastised the ambitions of
    The eyes that felt so sure

– But they declined to play the game
    The proud legs had begun,
And they could stare down anything
    Faster than legs could run.

Therefore the summer saw the legs
    Give up their cold disguise,
And sun themselves to frazzles for
    The catching of the eyes;

And thus it was the bolder eyes
    Could stare down easily
The flimsy ramparts of the legs,
    And have their victory,

Have it, have it and tire of it
    Much sooner than they thought,
And spend the autumn brooding on
    The truth the legs had taught:

That love is not as hard-won or
    As worthwhile as it looks,

And those that tell you differently
 Have only stared at books.

2. Ars Poetica

O here we go a-gathering
 The samphire from the crannies,
Inside the little baskets woven
 For us by our grannies.

Two hundred feet below, the rocks,
 And up above, the spaces,
And here the wind that thumps us while
 The rain runs down our faces.

Yet still we edge down clutching
 Special clippers to collect it,
Hoping to find it hanging out
 Where no one would expect it,

Looking to catch it unawares,
 All richly green, and blooming
Within our fingers' nimble grasp,
 Before it sees us coming.

If gathering rosebuds should be quite
 A profitable doddle,
And nuts in May might sell O.K.,
 Our samphire brings in sod-all;

But following daily such a dread-
 ful trade to earn a living,
With every second on that cliff
 So cruel and unforgiving,

Is fine – as long as no one comes
      And asks us what we do there . . .
We'd have to say, Without our toil,
      Just who would know it grew there?

3. Against Mathematics

O Sod sits up there on his bench,
      And when things are just awful,
Throws down some extra lumps of mud
      Pretending that it's lawful.

But though Sod's Law is petty, and
      Productive of frustrations,
In its odd way it does permit
      Of kindly deviations:

Where mathematics says *Man dies*
      Like all the other fauna,
Sod's quirky Law says *Live some more,*
      There's trouble round the corner.

Old Sod is sly but jocular
      – Plain fact and not a rumour –
But Maths by definition works
      Without a sense of humour;

And whereas Sod chucks mud with no
      Fixed rules for hour or season,
Maths functions logically by
      The ruthless clock of reason.

There is no mercy ever for
      The ones who starve in attics,
Victims of the inexorable
      Laws of mathematics,

But Sod at least has idle days
      When he provides some quarter
– And makes a happier study for
      Your able son; or daughter.

TEASHOP '92

O superfluous sprays of light on an esplanade!
The winter urn is cooling, the girl is closing:
I'm sorry, she says, *We are closing now.*

– But the customer asks about tea with such hope-less charm
That the girl is not resentful she cannot
Go home quite yet; perhaps go home any more.

This one can charm the birds down from the trees
So they thud to the ground in dozens, and the girl
Is second by second feeling wingless

– And she drops down behind the counter, behind
The fridge of coloured ices, small plastic skips
Full of scraped-at choices of lime, or tangerine,

Or rum-and-raisin. It drones while he drums his fingers
(Little finger up to thumb) and smiles and smiles.
The girl lies there and thinks, *Do I have a choice?*

With my head against the cartons of UHT?
With my eyes trapped by shelves lined by newspapers
Full of photographs of terrors I hadn't really

Ever noticed 'til this moment, one leg straight out,
One leg bent under, one thin arm free to move?
Could I lie here and hope he leaves, and closes

The door? she wonders. I shall know if he's gone
When the bell rings. Or should I push
The panic button, fast, for living help?

Or should I serve him? Over the sea, the sun
Goes through the bottom-line horizon, far away,
Below three colour-choices of January cloud.

MOSQUITO

Fancy this in October, the last
Mosquito of summer left buzzing alone,
Its last fling in my room on the sixth floor
Of a tower block hotel; marooned like one
In his seventh decade with only the past
To look forward to, as the one sure

Topic he can buzz round with some old chum.
'I had a good bloody summer,' it seems to say,
'With waiter and bellman, and that prim peach
Who keeps the consultant's books across the way.'
And for one last sally it swoops and bites my thumb.
So I bite mine back at it, and reach

For a folded newspaper; all the same aware
How much I resemble it, my own small spites
And hopeless needs reduced to the last fling
Of one who doles out charm in sexless bites
To check-out girls and bank clerks as if to swear,
'Oh man, I buzz and suck like anything!'

SUMMER TIME ENDS

How nice looking up, some cloudy afternoon,
To see that what has fallen suddenly
Is twilight, and an earlier chance to draw
The curtains while you have the energy.

Now everything falls, go down with it and give
Yourself to the gravity, putting up a show
Of warming wistfulness with the last leaves.
Fall hard, and stay there, waiting for the snow.

The nights are drawing in, nothing wrong with that.
The poet says: *Darkness cures what day inflicts.*
It is as normal to welcome winter back
As to loathe the spring. Popular interdicts

May forbid that preference, but snow walks are like
Illicit love with no one else betrayed;
Are like the joy, as you step out through the white,
Of the first alligator in the first everglade.

Harden your skin, then, for the rigorous spell
Between October and the April days
When the clocks go wrong again. Live for the thought
Of the bracing dark and the heavenly displays,

On frosty nights, of dotty groups of stars
You may sit and try to specify all night
– As if there were no tomorrow to dissolve
Their shining in dull anywheres of light.

SHE

The latest conclusion: *Drink* is rapidly
Acquiring a me problem. The girl I presume
Most of any day to follow, but don't meet at all
– Last thing at night she is actually in the room
As the large hours shift into the small,
Sitting over there and (*Sex* is obsessed with me)
Watching these lines take their particular
Shape as my latest tentative report
On all that she means; laughing too readily
While the halo of my table lamp stops short
Of her hair, which would indisputably
Shine with it, if it could ever reach that far.

THE BARON'S HORSE

So there was I, woken up on the airy height
Of an eighty-foot steeple by my master – the story goes –
Shouting up at me from below, *We must move on!*
It's eight o'clock, and we must be moving on,
And you're stuck up there tied to a past when the snows
Of faith were at the full – ten o'clock last night!

'But I'm happier here,' I neighed back, as my hoofs
Slid, and grappled at the slates, 'I've known far worse
Dilemmas and qualms than this, this feels like comfort
To a horse who has seen and suffered, it's more like comfort –'
I have the ultimate shit-scared, fundamental horse,
It seems! he thundered. Drips dropped from all the roofs

As he ranted with no regard for my situation,
Some eighty comforting feet above the town,

Still slithering after the thought of the one God,
Or any available prophet of the one God
– Until, with a shot, my master brought me down
To his earth again; and to pure imagination.

SEVEN SHERLOCKS

The man on the bus to the beach was Chinese.
He was certainly not. He was disguised
As a Chinese. Did you not see how he read
His little Li-Po edition from front to back?

But the only prints on the sand were those
Of a horse. – Or those left by a tall man
Taking careful strides with horseshoes attached
To the soles of cheap wellington boots.

So the third man in the saltmarsh was never
– *There at all?* Quite.Was never there at all.
Because he did not relax his guard and walk
Away. He stood still. He was a scarecrow.

And there was nothing wrong with the old red kiosk
Outside the village store. *But I think there was!*
No! Briggs was standing in it using
His mobile phone to *persuade* us that there was.

All that nodding and shaking of his bald head
At what Carstairs was saying . . . – Yes, messages
To his accomplice on the distant dunes.
He could do nothing when the sun went in.

And the vital missing *element, just*
As important as the rest? – The absence

Of a haystack near the gate. Had one been there,
He would have shoved our needle into it.

Then, you see, those clouds . . . They were *painted* on the sky
In the manner of the artist Magritte.
– *But how could you tell?* – On longer inspection,
I found crucial errors in the forgery.

RISK-TAKERS

Bad day, forecast *Sultry*, the flag
On the pole above the Russian
Roulette Club in the High Street limp,
Their bar shut, its blinds drawn, too few
Proven fatalities lately
To attract new members.
                       Try *Life*
Instead? With some rival outfit
Like *Aerobic Death Restriction?*
Well, you could all the same end up
With a craving for risk – years lost
You could have glutted on it.
                           No,
Cross the High Street, and take a look.
On the door of that place it says
Pleasant club requires risk-takers
Less gone on money than seeking
The hazards of high art.
                     The gun,
Primed by Amanda, Natalie,
Cindy (whoever's on duty
On the fateful week-end) has *pen*,
Or *stave, brush* or *chisel* sprayed in

Blood, sperm or tears on its barrel.
On the wall in the corner of
The agonized back saloon where
The baize table stands, among pinned
Banknotes with the price on each face,
You might find Benjamin Franklin
Looking jealous on his greenback:
The frown of power, yes; but scared white.

FACIAL

Inaccurate foray, in front of the bathroom mirror,
With blunt scissors angled too awkwardly near the eyes,
That see an infinite snow of hairs spread across
The sheet of white cardboard held widely under my chin . . .

I tap the edge of the card with the closed blades,
And all the hairs shift together like filings pulled
Into sentient activity by a magnet.
Dropped into the bathroom basin they cluster and clog

The outlet like a dampened pubic bush,
A mesh that looks wiry enough to scour the bowl with.
I pick up this excrement, a grey-brown ball
To flush, or dump in a bin, when I have finished;

But I can't say how long that will take, say how much longer
I should spare to go on attempting to reach a state
When I look just trim and suitable; not, as now,
More exposed and less composed than when I started.

SONNET IN SLOPPY JOE'S

A red-bead message runs all along the wall:
For the Best American Breakfast the Flame
-Grilled Burger, This is the PLACE. Lids of some tall
Coffee-pots with chrome knobs on look much the same
As Kaiser Wilhelm helmets; they don't make sense,
But they've used them by filling them up half-way
With clusters of coffee-bags, like a pretence
Of fungi on trees.

            And soon that girl will say,
'Mum, did you see that Tammy Wynette had died?
What will Grandma think?' – 'Oh, she knows already,
She heard it on the 6 a.m. news. She cried,
And said, "I think I'll have a glass of sherry."
But six is much too early for sherry, Mum.
"Not for me", she said. "Not for me." And she *had* some.'

AVALANCHE DOGS

At a whistling instruction from its trainer,
The little dog leapt at the large bank of snow,
Sniffed and barked and scratched, and its trainer helped it,
And through a hole they made the crowd could see
A face, that soon turned out to be Mrs Sundquist's.

My cat, and all my previous cats, have warned me
Against giving undue respect to any dog
Or credence to its talents. Did I listen too much?
This dog was thrown things for showing off its flair,
Though not many people seemed to value the sacrifice

Donated by Mrs Sundquist, who was covered
With snow again for a second dog to find her
– All this being done to show the ability
Of avalanche dogs to get Mrs Sundquist,
Or you or me perhaps, out of mountain snows,

In this case in the Lappland Arctic region,
Where every husky in the dog-sled teams
Knows left from right . . . And a third dog, and a fourth,
Mrs Sundquist being buried and reburied
Time and time again in the square outside People's House,

And people applauding the dogs, yet not Mrs Sundquist
When she finally came out from her hour-long incarceration
In the twilight drift.
                  I clapped my own soft gloves,
And one or two others took up the applause
– But which of us had brought anything to throw

To Mrs Anna Sundquist, dog's best friend?

TREES NEAR PODORAS

Not the same week every autumn, but the same
Place and surprise: clouds and clouds all day,
At six made over to encroaching dark
– And then this avenue which, for a spell,
We have driven along (planted by Communists
With the decent motive, that time, of providing
A windbreak on a windy plain) suddenly
Lights up our way through the dying afternoon,
As the breeze blows, turns, and flattens the leaves
On their yellow sides, so they provide a wide

Gold illumination, a rush of light.

It gives

A ceremonial radiance to a road
Which once more looks as if it still might offer
A future with possibilities. So does
The instinctive raised thumb of liberal well-wishing
From the shepherd, returning our wave of thanks
When he barred his bleating gang for our car to pass,
Folding down at the end into a fist of hope.

LEAVING THE WORLD OF PLEASURE

I gave up on the Mall of All Desires.
I thought it was pushing too much pleasure at me.

It was also other people's pleasure, thank you,
Not something I'd dreamed and chosen for myself.

They'd like to relaunch it for me, but they can't.
There's no new, lasting desire after twenty-five.

After the Mall, I saw the attraction of sorrow.
There was more scope in it for quenching old desires.

And it seemed to have a border, with happiness
On the unattainable other side of it.

INCIDENT ON A HOLIDAY

The cat between the tables is not worth attention,
But the most of *us* is closed in plastic now,
Magnetic so we stick to their powerful fingers.
I have to swipe to be a citizen.
I have to stand still while they target me.

Though one night on a coast of this vast and
Increasing inattention, a disco selling
Illusions to themselves for a sizeable profit
Goes up in flames in the small hours
– A blaze of interest on the coast opposite.

In this hinterland, however, no one explains it,
Not even the backstreet barber, the big
Conspiracy theorist, who avoids my eyes
In his pocked mirror; or the extrovert licensee
Working faster but very quietly, mopping his bar;

Not even the check-out girl taking one by one
The grapefruit rolled down in a ritual
To break the boredom of her dreadful day
And start her chatting – she doesn't as much as smile
When I ask her, 'Who would trash a lovely disco?'

– And claim the insurance on all the pretty dreams?
What sort of destructive decency? There was
No cc-tv watching, no bar code bleeped
When some unpoliced fingers scratched the match into flame.
And now there is a gap in the esplanade . . .

Though otherwise things go on pretty much the same:
The barber thanks me and tells me to Take Care,

The licensee puts my drink down – 'There you go!' –
The waters eject our pollution onto our shores,
And the cat, without e-mail, susses the customers

In the Sea Café, and refuses their burger bits.

KNOCK KNOCK

Do I need them? The glasses on my face?
The coat snatched to cover me? Not questions that I pose
Warm indoors while thinking *Nude is beautiful*,
But having unlocked the front door onto space,
And stared out into it to discover all
Of nobody there, and no neighbour to tell me whose

Loud knocking that might have been. I feel quite bold,
Because I don't shiver . . . Except I *can't*, my skin
Has suddenly felt content with nothing more
Than taking on, like clothes, the outer cold
– And the notion of re-shutting the opened door
Seems to be receding. With no one to let in,

I could go on standing in the freezing air
While my will to speak or move drained right away,
And the dark fastened hard on my illuminous
Nakedness. And then, if I called, 'Who's there?'
And heard – 'Bonaparte!' I'd say, 'Ridiculous!
Bonaparte *qui?*' . . . 'Bon appartement a louer.'

THE MEN AROUND HER BED

(2004)

SEPTEMBER 1939

I walked into the garden afterwards:

Away up there the soft silver elephants

        hovered   peculiarly

The wireless had gone over to
A band . . . Or a short feature?
Whichever, I didn't listen.

My mother listened on, half-listened on,
And was thinking, as she watched me from the window.
She told me that.

There was no one in the gardens on either side,
And I too thought: *It will be different now.*

The elephants' noses wrinkled in the breeze.

DIALOGUE OF THE BELIEVING GENTLEMAN AND THE ATHEIST MAID

The Gentleman:

> You crossed your legs and gave no reason why,
> A moment ago. We were talking about the high
>
> Implications of great art. I said 'They are religious',
> A point of view you called 'preposterous'.

But I love the St Matthew Passion, I love the Mo-
na Lisa, both of which surely show

The power of a Higher Being. Then George Herbert – he
Who chastised wealth and pomp and vanity –

His work, for me, is intrinsic, and surely God
Decreed that it should exist? To me it's odd

To find some – Well, to find a girl like *you*
Who doesn't have any inkling of the true

Religiousness of Great Art. – And one more thought begs
An answer still: Why did you cross your legs?

The Maid:

In bed with you I could cure you of God;
But that wouldn't be to deprive you of Michelangelo's
David, or of the Resurrection
Symphony (so named), or of the Holy Sonnets.
It's 'God' I'm banishing, not the works of man
(Or woman, naturally.) – Including your Gerard Manley
Hopkins, great nature poet.
                                        In bed we'd watch
Late dust coming in, as we'd leave a window open
To catch the pollen of the evolving flowers,
The dust from the roadworks, and from the crematoria
Cresting the bland peripheral hills of London
– Particles of our impermanency, but
Shot through with such infamy and pleasure, sent
Up by the tumult of the lovebeds where
Those who love love love Telemann as much.

SAYINGS OF THE UTOPIANS

In a neglected Utopian black-and-white film
Which dates from the nineteen-thirties, a beautiful
Young girl sits in a smart bright restaurant
To which she has been escorted by an old man.
He has a trim white beard and a cunning charm,
And one may assume he planned this carefully.
She had been alone in her cold, bare, silent room.
Here is warmth – and flowers, champagne – and a gypsy band.

Insofar as he is audible above
The deafening silken-shirted Utopian gypsies,
She is listening to him. He is saying, 'Every young woman
As beautiful as you should have three lovers:
A twenty-year-old for passion,
A forty-year-old for passion and experience,
And a sixty-year-old for passion, experience
– And wisdom' (thus the sub-titles render it).

She being a sharp-witted girl, as well
As a beautiful one, she rejoins, 'So which are *you?*'
He smiles, and is about to answer her question
With words of cunning charm that will change her future,
When the waiter interrupts them. He wants their order.
He is not the suave waiter you get in unreal films,
He is slow, and lethargic, and derives *no* interest
From the customers as a salve for his tedious task.

The timing has been ruined, the moment passes
And it can't be recovered. The old man does not seduce her,
She does not marry him and inherit millions
From his trade as an insurer; and launder them
Into a salon for young post-Dadaists.
To attain the ideal, first disperse all crude illusion.
The man who made this bitter-sweet comedy belonged
To the school of directors known as 'Utopian realists'.

ANITA 1944

This refers again to Anita, she
Who was in an earlier poem. We
Never spoke, and I wrote it without praise
Of all her grace among the bygone boys

In those 1940s . . . But to-night I can see her bike,
On the easy pedals of which she mounted high
And rode away from the gang up Shorndean Street.
See it once more, and recall how I dreamed the sleek

Style of her body for a long long while
Before I would think of dreaming it in rhyme.
– Now there revisits, too, her pregnancy
By a legal husband, and the memory

Of her managing a pram with the aid
Of her practical mother as day by day they made
Their way up the same street, the Mum advising,
Anita in the fold, submitting, dying.

Awful to save her as a vision of
Fulfilment that needed nothing approaching love,
Just the dark fumblings of insomnia
When the maths wouldn't come out . . . Then I think of her

As perhaps alive? – Yes. Thankfully unaware
That in these memories she needs to share
Commemoration with the ack-ack sites
That kept me more awake on late June nights.

THE SECRET HATS

O dentists, no need for your Santa Hats in August!

If you cannot love me in a corporate hat . . . then I'll remove it

Post coitum no market for hats with feathers

The wedding pics in the locals: the frigid veils, the bride-
grooms' trilbies past lust already

Near her traffic cushion, slow down for Tania raising her
champagne – her paper hat out of the Pisces cracker

Who was it held open the twentieth swing door in succession?
It has to be the gentleman in the black hat

Come out from that wall and put your lid on, post-box. Be a
pillar of real communication

'My apologies!' – Thus the passenger in the hat, as he answers
the mobile lent him against his wish

In fewer memories daily, Mariela's hat. All we ever saw above
the wall as she strode into the Bursary

When he started his new religion what hat did he wear? The
one that still means the worship of Wobbly Hats

The scattered ashes of my deerstalker friend as they plaster the
hated ground elder

With the skewer, make more holes in your belt. Here you need
both hands to hold your hat on in the wind

In the windy street, is the vendor's hat really holding down
    that pile of papers? Only with a stone inside

So why do they gather in coats and hats at the corner? To
    rename the street after a headgear guru

THROUGH GLASS

I have gone by too quickly for only
a second sharply catching the two men
through two walls of glass the bus window's
and the café's where they sit in a fierce crouch
facing each other with strip light falling
across their small glass cups as if there were
still something in them while one of the two
is lifting his own with hope in the silence of
their defeated staring down at a table top
itself made of glass but without a pattern
or anything underneath it to stare out
while outside the feet go patrolling past
at dawn and in twilight perpetually
towards what the two think close in on their short lives
like punctuation marks: satisfactions.

THE GHOSTLY REGIONS

There are some left, some ghostly, ghastly regions
    Crossed by stale stopping trains where many seats
Are occupied by pale purposeless poor, and by silent
    Unremembered girls found later dismembered

By Senior Citizens sauntering back from the bingo
　　In black bags in alleyways, or shallowly buried
In woodland frequented frequently by rapists
　　Descended from decent cheerful chapelgoers.

One such was Melissa, meticulous in arithmetic, always
　　Achieving praise for perfection when she presented sums
To the lovely Miss Wolfenden, weary at the teacher's task.
　　And she spelt superbly, and her geography projects
Were never less than neat, and chastely coloured.
　　She would settle down to be, and be seen to be,
A suitable silent spouse for a friend in her form,
　　It being obvious there was no better option.

It was not as if she was utterly unaware
　　Of her elder brother's brackish activities.
Insofar as she thought, she thought them unimportant.
　　So her parents placed her, they put her down with a frown
As a plain, private girl . . . she'd come to no horrible harm.
　　Not for her the coarse canal, near that banal
Locality called 'the Loveys' where local lovers
　　Would go and be mocked at by prurient-curious children . . .

– And one day Melissa was found – staying late in the Library
　　Rejecting the ruffian who avidly approached her
And rested a rigid hand on her shapely shoulder
　　Suggesting a droll little stroll in the brisk bright weather
To the worst of the hairy havens where all hope withered,
　　– Found with eyes down on Emily Dickinson, read with dread
For the first timely time – seized and studied,
　　To shake herself fatefully free of that breathing shadow.

A DAY IN 1966

I was ambling up from the Lower Annexe
– As distinct from the 'Upper' or 'First' Annexe built
With the flood of funding that also appointed me –
And along the covered uphill walkway between
The Library and the new Biology Lab
When I saw, as I passed the Senior Kitchen window,
The girl with her hair on fire.

The Principal Lecturer in Cookery, the President
Of the Junior Common Room, the Netball
Vice-Secretary and various beautiful
Young girl – or 'woman' – students (as we were starting
To describe them) were just standing round and looking
– That being the one-tenth second in which
They had heard the howl, and turned, and seen

But hadn't moved. Oh god, Jane's hair,
Is a scream of flame – I have to reach –
Reach her – All they do is stand and watch.
And then I am pushing through the heavy outer door
Of the Senior Kitchen, and through the lobby where
The coats are left, and Jane's howling head
Is being smothered in a coarse white apron

Grabbed from a proximate peg by Victoria
At the Principal Lecturer's shouted instruction.
– Out of which Jane's face comes finally
In a sudden trembling rictus of distress
I have seen before, but might not say when or why,
And with an indrawn Oh of astonishment
Staring at me. And what am I doing there?

THE PRESENTATION

She becomes aware of the men around her bed
– The four of them edging up with blue,
Mauve, red and yellow bunches – when one has said,
As she opens her eyes and is plainly seeing them,
'There you go, young woman, all for you
With our love and thanks. Get well, Deb – soon!'
The hem

Of the scarlet curtain doesn't keep out the sun
At half-past five; so she wants it pulled, and that
Is done by one. One unwraps the flowers. And one
Goes for scissors to do surgery on the stalks.
Then the cheerfullest, the fourth, in his bobble hat,
Leans down to kiss her, after which he walks

Away up the ward to fetch vases so that each
Can fill and arrange a vase and lodge it there
On her locker, brightly. Then they smile and reach
A hand out, one by one, to her warm long hand,
And stand back to attention, a rigid pair
On either side of her.
We can understand

How they all thought this could have been a funeral
They'd come to say goodbye at – but oh, was not –
With the flowers and that; then it sneakily came to all,
And at the same moment, that this was about Life
– Which Deb was for enhancing . . . And so what,
If every man there had a job, and wife?

Hell, for an hour they'd switched their meters off.

TALKING ANIMALS

Why don't we lie here and make up
New animals, I said to her;

Not thinking that – not consciously –
It was a blatant metaphor.

She left me. And she went and had
Liaison with another chap,

Which in the course of thirteen years
Put various creatures on the map

Who, yes, were new, and animals,
But not the sort I would invent . . .

– One's dead, one's rich, and one's still at
The University of Kent.

PAROLE
(i.m. I. H.)

The lately dead still arrive in the corner of your eye
Past the restaurant window, preparing slow smiles of pride
At achieving their return. They know that without them
You can never be the same, so they cheat for a while.
They keep trying to work a parole to the usual places,
They won't be excluded from them if you are there.

Their fingers have pressed the latch and the door nearly opens,
But then their smile turns embarrassed because they find
It behaves like a turnstile: they think they have admission,

But this door is fixed to prevent them coming back in.
And you just can't help, at all; if you went out to greet them
They would not be there, no one in the street would have seen them.

Then slowly the corner of your eye
Forgets to look.

ANAC 2004

Suddenly into the hugeness of the Tourist Hotel
Arrive three-hundred-and-twenty archaeologists,
The Annual National Archaeological Congress.
                                        At breakfast,
I ask in faltering parody of their language,
'Why are you here?' 'To excavate an ancient historical site,'
Is the reply of the man whose badge reveals
He is 'Professor Szkrvzc'.

                              One local paper
Writes with a similar message. The other rag,
The organ of the other ethnicity,
Says, 'That's a lie, faithful readers. They are here
In an arrantly dishonest endeavour to prove
That this terrain was, in the earliest times, the home
Of the ancestors of the present minority,
Who thus can claim it as theirs, old pots and sherds
Will show it beyond doubt, that's what they hope . . .'

I ask no more questions of individuals,
But next day go and stand in unseasonal rain,
And watch the insistent digging going on
In the search for ancient tools and artefacts
Made with much more desire to cultivate, and eat,

Than to validate future boundaries,
And watch their eyes as they prise away hard clay
From potentially momentous bits and pieces,
Or just other hunks of harder ancient clay,
And listen in case there are sudden cheers (which there aren't)
At discovering something wonderful which provides
A much-desired political revelation

– And recall the words Albert Camus used in
A story I used to read to grammar school boys
Fifty years ago, before the latest troubles,
Though long after Hamlet's father and the Polacks
Went out on the frozen wastes to smite each other,
With many articulate sons dead because of that:
Camus on the 'rotten spite, the tireless hates,
The blood lust of all men'.

COLLECTED POEMS
(2006)

poems not in individual volumes

OVERLAPS

For twenty-two years it was the Old Dog Restaurant.
For twenty-two years Karl stood at the door by the dog
To welcome you in and show you to Lula's tables.
Young impressionists crowded into the Old Dog.

One day without notice it was the New Dog Bistro,
With new, smiling dog, no welcome and different decor;
But Lula still worked there so I stayed with it.
Old Karl was in the background and I was happy.

New people sat at the beautiful Loramine's tables,
They were post-impressionists.
                                    Then after sixteen years
It refurbished as the Brand New Hound Attitude:
No dog, no service, fast food through a hatch;

Though Loramine, in charge, kept Lula who remembered Karl
And didn't get on with the neo-Brit nihilists
Who more or less carved up the place for about four years.
Until – Well then I myself stopped going back…

Some managing hand had managed to hand it on
To a lifestyle beyond description or definition,
A dysfunctional game-plan that linked with nothing before
And wanted nothing after, an anti-dog mode.

I had spent three adolescences in thrall
To those three regimes, no wish for a fourth
Without Karl, without Lula, without even Loramine
And the dogbite scar on her left leg, above the knee.

The place is still part of me, as 'my spiritual home'.
Though the food when you ate it was lousy, it did become

More edible with nostalgia.

                                 I see old Loramine
And she often recalls 'dear Lula, dear old Karl.' I say,

'Like me, you need overlaps to go on living.'

MARECHIARE,

By Tosti. Lousiest of love songs, and on Radio Three
At that! But my finger pauses an inch
Away from the button because I've remembered something.
I've remembered my daily journey to that school
In the late nineteen-fifties, with that colleague

In the same eight-seat compartment, smog-stained windows,
Soiled upholstery, seaside pictures, Elmers End,
Eden Park, West Wickham, Hayes. All the time,
My companion, the cynical music master,
Would drone and hum and smile and apologise

– Lesson preparation. The suburban landscape
Would modulate through Macmillan's constituency
From inner to outer, and 'You could call that *countryside*,
For a yard or two,' he'd say. And throughout one week,
When we had the Parents' Evening on the Friday,

Having sung at Glyndebourne, and being capable
Of presenting himself as a decent *tenore robusto*,
He practised Tosti's ballad for the Parents,
Its fustian intro, its maudlin vocal acrobatics . . .
The windows rattled on their leather straps.

Scrubland with never-inhabited workshop ruins.
Golf-course with flags in holes on pallid greens.
– He practised for the Parents as it all went by,
'And who *cares*! Honestly, Brownjohn, who fucking *cares*!'
He would say, with the formality of the age.

At Elmers End, if I'm right, on the Friday morning,
With 'another day opening its squalid legs
For us to squander ourselves in', he got out,
And 'not to ruin your entire bloody journey', he
Climbed into the next compartment, which was empty.

– But now I'm back in the present, my pausing finger
Still allowing the song to go on to its awful end
On the radio fifty years later; and I believe
I can still hear him singing over the slow wheels
That carried us on to a place he said 'didn't deserve us',

His howling impassioned tenor heard through a wall
On which they'd put, as in most of those compartments,
A mirror, a small clear mirror, for combing
Your hair in or pulling your face into shapes
Better suited to facing interviews or girlfriends

Or just teaching spelling . . .Which I see myself in today,
As I was at twenty-six and am no longer;
And I find I'm crying at these two swooping voices,
Jim Farr's and Tito Schipa's, reminding me
That like Tosti's fishes I go on 'gasping for love.'

A SCREAM IN 1890

A scream in the room that goes on for ever, long
Tidy table after table into the distance, my grandmother
Pedals harder suddenly, and stops.
Any time you stopped, you looked at the clock and wondered
Can I rest for a moment and still catch up with the work?
This is five-and-twenty to nine, she remembers
Fifty-two years on.
                    The scream has come
From a girl a long way behind her, a needle
Has gone through somebody's thumb several tables back.
– First, a second so quiet that you could have heard a –

Then other screams, like late echoes. The girl looks at
The thumb pinned down as if it wasn't hers.
Girls from elsewhere crowd round her, they always
Said it would happen, most girls knew someone who'd done it,
It was when you were tired – but then you were always tired.
Why should careful Flora have done it?
                         The overseer
(She thinks it was the word) shoves them all aside –
'Get back to work. No talking!' And takes a look
At the girl, at the thumb, at the blood
Spreading under the nail in the nineteenth-century sunlight.

Obediently no one talks, but they seize
Sidelong glances at each other and sit still.
They can hear his words in the silence before resuming,
Their eyes all going back to their own thumbs.
They can hear what he says, and will always remember the tone
Mr Podmore the overseer uses, applying
The discipline of his own overseers, telling Flora:
Move the wheel   *listen* to me   move it *yourself*
Move it very slowly   slowly   as slowly
As you can   that's it   that's it   Are you all right?

LUDBROOKE AND OTHERS
(2010)

Ludbrooke

HIS MORNING – I

Something rotates his upper half anti-clockwise
Roughly ninety degrees to the left, and his legs overhang
The sanded and polished floorboards he hoped might lift
His morale for a new millennium. Now his eyes,
Which he opens after one or two aerobics,
Can face the wardrobe where twelve laundry hangers
Preserve his dry-cleaned image in a dark cave
The moths have demoted as not worth researching.
An unconscious force has pushed and pulled him outwards
Into another day draining his morale
By a few more drops, if he allows it. He will *not*.
He will take some vigorous action, the simple fact
That he can still stand up makes him optimistic.

HIS 1471

No one has phoned him for what seems several days.
Ludbrooke tries one-four-seven-one, the lonely man's friend,
And confirms it, his last call was on the ninth.
'The caller withheld "their" number.' The adjective 'their'
Annoys the pedantic Ludbrooke, who detects yet another
Example of political correctness. If only
A plural of persons *were* phoning Ludbrooke.
The message suggests it was a commercial call.
The commercial callers hate people to phone back,
People might ring back who hate being targeted.
Sometimes Ludbrooke would love to be targeted
He imagines the short skirt of the targeter walking
Home from the call centre with her mobile off.

HIS SCENERY

Visible from his back window in London N.2
Is a said-to-be Chinese knocking-shop; he has seen
A to-ing and fro-ing with some regularity
Of 'slim and elegant' classified-ads girls daily
From early afternoon to late at night.
He won't give it a try.
                          But he does wonder
What on earth could be the Chinese term for
The gentle, purposeful tapping at the door
When the fifteen minutes is up (which, of course,
Gives knocking-shops their name)?
                                  And later thinks
Of a pale pliant hand softly making arrive
Exquisitely and fast a tiny little
Ideogram for that for him for him.

HIS STAND-UP – I

'I got sexual abuse every day when I was a kid.
Every day my father would say, What's that
Little fucker doing now? Reminds me of the one about – about' –
[Be aware that this is Ludbrooke's audition] –
'About the two guys who – the two guys who' – [Ludbrooke has
Forgotten the link!] 'the one about the doorbell
Ringing in a brothel' [Ludbrooke's confidence
Returns as he sees they are listening] 'and on the step
Is a man in a wheelchair, no arms, no legs' –
[He remembers to say 'Which isn't funny really'. It gets
A laugh] – 'and the madam says, Well are you really –
Do you *really* – ? And the guy says, Well . . . I rang the bell, didn't I?'
Thank you, Mr –? Mr Ladbrooke? We'll be in touch.

HIS ASPIRATION

Ludbrooke desires an honorary degree,
'Desires' being stronger than 'wants' and a euphemism
For 'covets' or 'lusts after'. Is he taking
Ambition to the wire to expect the same honour
As some merely 'famous' crap-merchants like the lead guitar
In 'The Sordid Syndrome'? No, he is not. But the fact
That the lead guitar was doctored should have cancelled his lust
– And it didn't . . . He still wants an honorary degree . . .
Approaching his eighties and undoctored, Ludbrooke
Would accept one from even the New University
Of Leatherhead, for sixty toiling years
At his underpaid vocation.
                                    Ludbrooke suffers
From an MTD: Vanity – a Media-Transmitted Disease.

HIS MULTICULTURALISM

Shows in the delicate way he rests his head
– Despite every fear that she will remove it –
On the shoulder of Miss Chiang to watch *Duck Soup*,
The video, from his reproduction sofa.
The alarm clock rings beside the bed of the man
Made President with the aid of American money
In the shape of Miss Margaret Dumont, and the lovely Miss Chiang
Is completely puzzled by Mr Groucho Marx.
'This gentleman – he is really *President?*' she asks.
Ludbrooke needs to lift his romantic head
To look at her, and answer. As he tries to explain
That this is not quite like life, her mobile rings;
As it does three times on the way back to Finchley Central.

HIS ABSTEMIOUS PHASE – I

Begins with a dinner of steamed vegetables,
Arranged round a fishcake eaten to mark
The Reduced Price sell-by-date on which
It went into his freezer one month before.
It's a Saturday, he could leave the washing-up,
But when he returns to his chair he has done it all,
Stacked it up in the kitchen cabinet, slammed the door,
And resorted again to his lengthening pencil list
Of the ways of restructuring a muddled life.
One is this: to consider four files retrieved
From a 'dedicated' drawer, three dating back
A year or two, the fourth new – and slim; and promising.
He sips a brew of resented herbal tea.

HIS ABSTEMIOUS PHASE – II

Concludes with this fourth file; preserving the one card
That came in response to three nervous letters,
And ending with the word they had agreed
Might finish a loving message in her own language.
But since he can't clearly read what preceded it,
He can't tell if it's sincere, or a joke sent
In whimsical recall of their single meeting
On that train long halted in a mountain tunnel.
They were alone in the eight-seat compartment.
They smiled. Ludbrooke courteously opened
His bottle of star-fruit liqueur, the national drink,
And they shared a few sips from its cap . . . Now he goes
To the kitchen for a tumbler, and drains the rest.

HIS CLASSIC MODESTY

This is my bedroom, he says in a casual voice,
*And lo, my bed, below my photograph
Of the Acropolis.* (My love-making, he thinks,
And sometimes even dares to say all this out loud
*Is like the Acropolis, an edifice
Wonderful to have experienced even once,
And transformative to have known for a little longer.
Sufficient of the Acropolis remains
In its incomparable magnificence
To stir a sensitive girl for years to come.
Those who forego it weep at what they have missed
When their chance has vanished.* And then he adds
Intelligent girls adore *the Acropolis.*)

HIS JEALOUSY

Ludbrooke doesn't practise jealousy. He
Has perfected it, deconstructed it, and junked it.
Impersonal tolerance rules. *Let them flirt
With whomever they like, I am indifferent.*
– Olympian, he waits for his latest to return
To his side at a particularly nasty party.
But she doesn't return.

                              He looks for her and finds her.
She moves away smiling, as if she hasn't seen him.
She is small, and very beautiful.
Ludbrooke is tall but he can't make out whether
She is still in the room. *Is she still in the bloody room?
Is her anorak still on the hook in our hostess's hall?*
– Nothing like jealousy for making you feel younger.

HIS TEMERITY

He would like to have done what the man did in the film,
When he left the woman's flat and went downstairs,
Then suddenly turned and tiptoed up again
And 'pressed his ear to the door' for twenty minutes,
Being able to hear all they said after he had gone
– Then finally, with footsteps audible inside,
Stayed in that same position as the door opened
And was discovered lurking but not embarrassed.
The man in the film just stood there guiltlessly smiling,
While the eavesdropped couple gasped and stared at him
With the certainty he had heard what he should not have.
He would like to have done it like the man in the film,
But it needed boldness, luck, and a thin door.

HIS BREAK

Always too knackered to remember what he packed
And the suitcase he used, he stands at the carousel letting
Some bizarre unwieldy thing go past
Three times before he says, *Sod it – that one's mine!*
He has finally seen the label to be his own,
Its illegible scrawl, its origin in
A travel agency bankrupt some months past;
And he has to stand and wait now for its fourth circuit,
Coming back by itself as if all the bags around it
Had shrunk away in immaculate disgust.
In his dream that night, all the travellers waiting with him
Are young women cramped with convulsive, unpleasant laughter
When he lunges to grab at this symbol of himself.

HIS TRAVELS – I

He books into a half-a-star hotel
In a non-cathedral city. Her mobile is off.
Whose mobile? He goes to their once-favourite
Restaurant where he half expected to dine her.
She does not show up. And this place only serves wine
By the bottle. So, never mind, he'll take
What he doesn't manage back to his hotel room
– Except he won't, the waitress has binned the cork
And pours constant fill-ups, soon he's drunk the lot.
The evening, like many others, away or home,
Is a stuporous failure, it founders in a mire
Of unworthy effort. But can he say, *Serve me right?*
No, he can't. (Whose mobile? His latest-before-last's.)

HIS TRAVELS – II

When he checks out, the man who takes his laundry
Is at Reception sorting out bills and receipts.
He is man of cultural refinement
Who can summon up a disarming turn of phrase:
'I see we're still washing your Oxfam shirt, sir.
It has seen better days – few of them with you.'
It occurs to Ludbrooke that if, like any other
Civilised man, he keeps a graded list
Of his larger garments (stopping short of what
The hotel calls 'private items') and changes one when
It falls below C+, he should listen
To this man regarding this shirt, which he now wears
To go home in, having awarded it a B.

HIS MORNING – II

His walk to the kitchen is an act of valour
That few could manage with the same *aplomb*
– Or so he tells himself with an outdated noun
From boys' adventure stories, where among those
Who possess it is the wounded scout not flinching
Before the surgeon, the leader who knows what to do
In the jungle ambush, the School cricket captain
No one guessed was the heir to a Balkan throne.
– Though it could be applied to a scoundrel: 'With insolent
Aplomb he picked up the duelling pistol.' Ludbrooke
Would accept any role that gave him what he finds
In Chambers' Dictionary after his lemon tea:
'Perpendicularity, self-possession, coolness.'

And Others

MY CRICKET

Began with watching war-stricken soldiers play
At a military hospital where I – if you please! –
Was a guinea-pig patient having his blood replaced
As a possible cure for childhood allergies.
On a makeshift wicket in the grounds, on a calm day
Of collateral sunshine, Wilson faced
Deliveries from Todd, with Baxter his runner ready
– And blocked ball after ball. Down in the book
Went platoons of diagonal pen-strokes, filling
Neat box after box – until that sudden hook,
Wilson's only stroke, dispatched his steady
Partner with bat thrust forward, willing

His own lame leg to win them a safe run.
When he'd reached the crease, Wilson would join him there,
Hobbling slowly down to wait for his next chance,
Which would come without warning as soon as one
Loose ball in about four overs provided a fair
Opportunity for scoring. From his grim trance
Of concentration, Wilson would suddenly
Emerge, open his shoulders – and eight – nine – ten
Came up in slammed singles made when he'd seen a gap
In the legside field, Baxter judging exactly when
He should start to lurch forward doggedly
Down the uneven pitch. Those two could wrap
A game up one run at a time, achieving
Through sheer persistence what other men would try
To accomplish by risk and daring and get nowhere.
Sixty-six years on I remember them, and lie
Awake in the blacked-out ward, with bombers leaving
Overhead for Cologne, and still can't bear
To imagine their futures. I myself left half-cured
Of my ailments by rigorous exercise with their drill-
Sergeant in the gym, which I had to attend
For my own rehabilitation. Did their firm will
Mean they recovered strength enough to be assured
Of more horrors, in desert or jungle? Or in the end,
Did they simply limp away, declared exempt
From extra bloodshed, to die in saner places?
I've tried in vain to work out how some can let
Life's harsh deliveries hurtle towards their faces,
And either ignore them, or clobber them with contempt.

Some things you never learn but can't forget.

ODE TO INSOMNIA

You are the queen of opportunities, the chance
To stumble and grope in refrigerated light
For the crust of sliced wholemeal in a plastic wrap,
And spread it with honey to finish in the dark
– Or to answer a letter with a purposeful
Clarity daytime would hedge and qualify.

– Or just to take up the headphone offer
Of *Turandot* or whatever . . . Don't believe
I worship you with despairing twists and turns,
I come to you straight. And when worship falters,
It's with waves on endless beaches, or the rotation
Of cakes in a somewhere strip-lit cavern of glass.

THE DUST

The silence was different because the sounds
Before it had been different. It grew deeper
With every new bend in the upward road
Through the parched mountain forest; until

I began to hear, where the track steepened,
Turned suddenly uphill and straightened out,
Sounds entering my ears from higher still,
Something bearing down on me from above,

Checking speed by braking on bend after bend,
Coming nearer with every step of my threatened life
On this upward venture into more and more dust,
On a stony track in another hottest summer.

Then the truck arrived with its grey bridal train of dust
On the straight itself, ten seconds up ahead.
I stood still on the only ledge above
A deep green drop that might have checked a fall,

And raised a hand, smiling, to a windscreen where
Another hand raised itself, someone smiling back
Acknowledging me, and leaving me again
Looking down alone through a settling cloud

At the shuddering cargo of logs that had been trees,
Each longer than the length of the truck itself;
At the end of the very largest, no white- or red-
Or any-coloured rag to warn about what it carried.

THE GRAVITY

now he is going to
fall and his hand goes out to
a fence but he wrenches the
whole thing out of
the ground and he staggers and
grabs at a post which
collapses and carries him
over the bank of
the river he hadn't
noticed was there, its
dry mud verge is almost as
hard as any stone for
falling on and he might
have gone over but for the
fence and the post and his stag-
gering in the hope he

would regain his balance and
not be destined as soon as
this to go down with
the gravity with the gravity

OF A FINANCIAL SCANDAL

It hit the fan at approximately eight-fifteen,
On a day in that terrible October,
And sprayed all over the latest *haute couture*

– Which was seen, when the screams died down, to have survived.
All the talk initially was about the dreadful s.
Bu the s. was soon forgotten.
                                And the fan slowed down

Until its individual blades could be seen
Going round with solid confidence. So the talk
Reverted to all the old topics, a voice remarking,

See, it's stopped altogether, now it's all right again.

OF THE LITTLE HEADS

It was one thing to have the car door opened
So he could step out into the daily crowd;
And one thing to have the heads around his neck

Blue purple yellow black soft and deferential,
Bestowing importance on each chosen word
– And another to wake up one morning and find them gone,

His perpetual necklace scattered invisibly
Over the colourless ground of a world
Where he drove all the way by himself, switched off

And stepped out alone again. Alone into no one.

OF A REQUIREMENT

There came a voice intoning compliments:
'You have led – how shall I say? – a *magnanimous* life,
Been self-effacing, generous and strong.

So you will be rewarded, despite the fact
That reward was never your object in behaving
In the principled fashion you have. There remains

Only one thing you must do. To comply
With the customary procedures, please click on
And follow the links, and – where requested – enter

The invoice for your fee plus any expenses'.

DRINKING SONG

I heard a lonely man in a bar
Sing *Here's to animals!*
– Unwittingly toasting every she
In a nearby Girls' Academy.
(Chorus of Professors:)
    If he had felt any tremor of doubt
    He could have left some of our students out,
    Not all are perfect. But he didn't.
    So – all together now – *Here's to animals!*

I heard a hungry man in a bar
Sing *Here's to vegetables!*
– Unknowingly praising every root
Or stalk or bough that provided fruit.
(Chorus of Ecologists:)
    If he'd been liable to pick and choose,
    He would have been content to lose
    A few examples. But he wasn't.
    All together now – *Here's to vegetables!*

I heard a sturdy man in a bar
Sing *Here's to minerals!*
– Rejoicing in all the age-long stayers,
Alps and Andes and Himalayas.
(Chorus of Geologists:)
    If he hadn't adored every rock and stone
    He should have left some of them alone,
    They're hazardous. But he couldn't.
    All together then, *Here's to minerals!*

I heard a distant man in a bar
Sing *Here's to the cosmos!*
– Lauding everything, near and far,
Near a big black hole in an ultimate bar.

(Chorus of Astrophysicists:)
>He need not have relished each particle
>And force as the genuine article,
>But he did just that. All together now –
>Here's to him – and here's to you –
>And *Here's to the cosmos*, through and through!
>Drink – drink – drink – to all of it,
>And stay away from the black black pit.

PRINTSHOP 1922: A TRUE MOMENT

The General Secretary of the Union
Turns up one Monday morning without notice,
As he prefers. The Works Manager allows him
To walk the shopfloor talking to the workers;
He could hardly, once in a while, refuse him this.

The General Secretary (quietly, but others can hear him)
Greets young Albert Whitaker with these words:
'Are you a member of my Union?'
'Yes, sir.' 'So are you proud to be?' 'Sir! – *yes*.'
'Then you'll wear a clean collar and tie at your machine.'

MR BANISTER

Our chemistry master, Mr Banister
(Not his real name) had only the one arm.
When the test tube cracked in the roarious flame
Of the bunsen burner, he replaced it four times
One winter afternoon. At the fifth attempt

Things went well enough for him to turn to the board
And with the one hand write up the formula
For his modest success.
                              Sometimes
He was slow up the stairs and we sat more quietly
Than at other times fearing his fury,
If he heard any noise as he turned the corner,
And limped along the top floor corridor
To growl his way into the lab that still
Returns in dreams (and why?)
                              Mr Banister
Hated teaching us, I think. 'Get *on* with something'
Was the phrase he used when he didn't want
To teach us anything at all, and sat on the stool
Behind the bunsen burner, the sink, the tap,
And in front of an empty board, as the light failed
Reading Simenon, the first time I'd ever heard
Of this author, whom I took to be a chemist.
The book he held in his hand was called *Lost Moorings*.

DECEMBER 31ST 2009

I step down in dying light
From the table on which I stood
On this last day of a decade
Screwing in a low energy bulb,
A token of somebody's scheme
For empowering me to be good,
And to play my part in small ways.
But the online newscasts reveal
Hour by hour how the larger thieves
Go on playing a different game
To pollute and cloud over our days.

The nought years have gone to their end
Like supplements gladly thrown in
With spent bottles and cartons and cans
To a good Green Citizen's bin.
The media historians
Will recount to us how we all lived,
The garments Celebrity wore,
The musics we should have preferred,
And which reputations survived
An acclaim they did not deserve.
But we already know the score.

When the bulb has brightened, I read
In hard-copy broadsheets of wars
That extended and raged unresolved,
Of treaties saluting the need
For the brokers of power to stay rich.
Through these last ten years famine gripped
Regions out of humanity's reach.
The measures we could have applied
To plant hope in a field of defeats
Went ignored, were the drowned-out song
Of long marches down monitored streets.

However you try, it's a task
To retrieve fast-vanishing fact
From among coloured spreads which maintain
'All you want is our visual world,
We permit you to see but not learn,
And not think – and above all, not act.'
In ingenious graphics, a dance
Of computerised death fills the screens
Where the language of management rules,
Cloaked in mantras which conceal
The crimes of its ignorance.

Though my writing's a hapless scrawl
Compared with four decades ago,
It might serve to cite one surprise
From the final hours of this year:
In a train stopped by seasonal snow
On a Circle Line platform, all eyes
Leaving tabloid headlines to fall
On the middle of nowhere, most hands
Clamped on cellphones, this occurred:
Something moved in front of our feet
Where we sat in dull silence – a bird.

Through doors open wide to the air
Where we'd halted at Edgware Road
(Perhaps to find out where we were)
The creature hopped in and patrolled
Past our bags as it foraged for crumbs.
Then the voice called, 'Doors closing, the train
Is about to depart.' All it had
Was its grey urban wings, to fly out
At around waist level and scare
Waiting 'customers' – landing again
Near a flickering platform ad.

It was not out to symbolise
The shortness of all our lives
With this three minutes exercise,
It just took its liberty
Of renouncing our heedless faces,
Getting out while the going was good,
Not desiring to stay on and be
Conveyed to too many more places
Where you clicked on Democracy
To find Freedom was a strict law
And Choice was compulsory.

Knowing what it was all about,
It appeared to forsake the entire
Shebang of our twenty-first
Century of terror and doubt.
– And its call was important to us.
There were wisdoms we might acquire
From its take on our decade's events:
When such powerful evils desire
To target us with their own aims,
Could we not ourselves form a flock
Migrating to common sense?

Are the limits of reason reached, where
Affirmation may only be said
To exist in football chants,
In New Year sieges of stores,
In flagged-up parades of the dead?
Has each truly affirmative cause
Become a mere shrug of despair?
I am sorry to fear, now it's dark,
That only the worst lies ahead;
Though the least we could show from now on
Is an odd affirmative spark.